That Field of Blood

THE BATTLE OF ANTIETAM
SEPTEMBER 17, 1862

by Daniel J. Vermilya

EMERGING CIVIL WAR SERIES

Chris Mackowski, series editor
Christopher Kolakowski, chief historian

The Emerging Civil War Series

offers compelling, easy-to-read overviews of some of the Civil War's most important battles and stories.

Recipient of the Army Historical Foundation's Lieutenant General Richard G. Trefry Award for contributions to the literature on the history of the U.S. Army

Also part of the Emerging Civil War Series:

For a complete list of titles in the Emerging Civil War Series, visit www.emergingcivilwar.com.

Also by Daniel J. Vermilya:

THE BATTLE OF ANTIETAM
SEPTEMBER 17, 1862

by Daniel J. Vermilya

EMERGING CIVIL WAR SERIES

SB
Savas Beatie
California

First edition, first printing

ISBN-13 (paperback): 978-1-61121-375-1
ISBN-13 (ebook): 978-1-61121-376-8

Names: Vermilya, Daniel J., author.
Title: That Field of Blood : the Battle of Antietam, September 17, 1862 / by Daniel J. Vermilya.
Description: First edition. | El Dorado Hills, California: Savas Beatie, 2018. | Series: Emerging Civil War series
Identifiers: LCCN 2017020855| ISBN 9781611213751 (pbk.) | ISBN 9781611213768 (ebk.)
Subjects: LCSH: Antietam, Battle of, Md., 1862.
Classification: LCC E474.65 .V47 2017 | DDC 973.7/336--dc23
LC record available at https://lccn.loc.gov/2017020855

SB

Published by
Savas Beatie LLC
989 Governor Drive, Suite 102
El Dorado Hills, California 95762
Phone: 916-941-6896
Email: sales@savasbeatie.com
Web: www.savasbeatie.com

Savas Beatie titles are available at special discounts for bulk purchases in the United States by corporations, institutions, and other organizations. For more details, please contact Special Sales, P.O. Box 4527, El Dorado Hills, CA 95762, or you may e-mail us at sales@savasbeatie.com, or visit our website at www. savasbeatie.com for additional information.

For Private Elwood Rodebaugh, 106th Pennsylvania Volunteer Infantry
Killed at Antietam, September 17, 1862

"Not for themselves, but for their country"

Joshua 1:9
Have I not commanded you? Be strong and courageous. Do not be afraid;
do not be discouraged, for the Lord your God will be with you wherever you go.

Table of Contents

Bibliography for this volume is available at
http://emergingcivilwar.com/publications/the-emerging-civil-war-series/footnotes

List of Maps

Maps by Hal Jespersen

Acknowledgments

A modern-day photo looks toward the observation tower from the Sunken Road. (cb)

There are many individuals who deserve thanks and credit for their help with this project. My editor, Chris Mackowski, has been extremely helpful throughout the process of writing and editing, and I'm very grateful to him and everyone at Savas Beatie. Hal Jespersen has yet again been wonderful to work with, producing first-rate maps for this book.

I also would like to thank my friends and colleagues of the National Park Service from Antietam National Battlefield and Gettysburg National Military Park. Caitlin Brown graciously helped by taking photographs of the battlefield, and this book would not be the same without her. John Hoptak authored a foreword for the book that perfectly captures why Antietam still stands as a landmark battle of the war, and why it was a powerful Union victory. Brian Baracz wrote an appendix on the history of Antietam National Battlefield, reminding readers of how Antietam has become the pristine, well-preserved battlefield that it is today. John and Brian also each read the manuscript and provided important feedback that made this a much better book. I also want to thank Keith Snyder, Alann Schmidt, Mike Gamble, and many others at Antietam, including my fellow battlefield guides there. I have had the chance to work alongside some very fine people and some of the best public historians in the country. I am indebt-

Stone sentinels from the Pennsylvania Reserves stand watch along Mansfield Avenue. (cm)

ed to them all for their knowledge and friendship.

Last, but not least, I would like to thank my family. My parents took me to Antietam for the first time when I was nine years old, and I have been fascinated by the battlefield ever since. My mom and dad have always given me unconditional support in all my endeavors, and I am very blessed to have them as my parents. My wife, Alison, has been my best friend, my most ardent proofreader, and my partner on many adventures. She makes every day better, and I could not be more thankful for her.

PHOTO CREDITS: Caitlin Brown (cb); Chris Mackowski (cm); Dan Vermilya (dv); Kevin Pawlak (kp); Library of Congress (loc); National Park Service (nps)

For the Emerging Civil War Series

Theodore P. Savas, *publisher*
Chris Mackowski, *series editor*
Christopher Kolakowski, *chief historian*
Kristopher D. White, *editor emeritus*

Sarah Keeney, *editorial consultant*
Maps by Hal Jespersen
Design and layout by H.R. Gordon
Publication supervision by Chris Mackowski

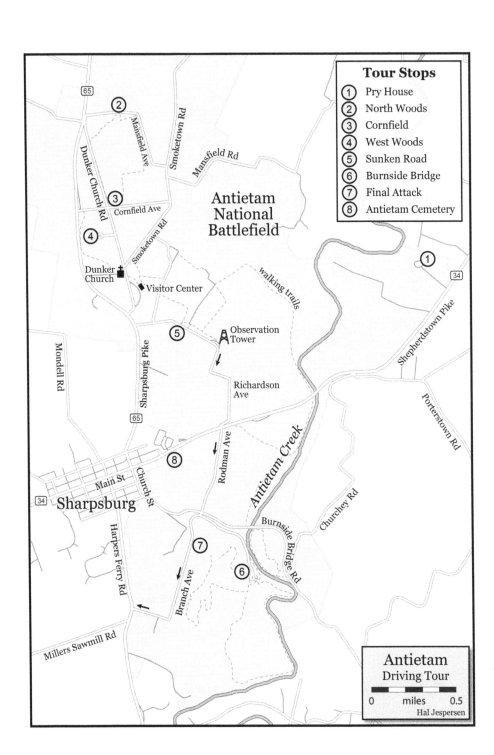

Tour Stops

1. Pry House
2. North Woods
3. Cornfield
4. West Woods
5. Sunken Road
6. Burnside Bridge
7. Final Attack
8. Antietam Cemetery

Antietam
National
Battlefield

65

Mansfield Ave

Smoketown Rd

Mansfield Rd

Dunker Church Rd

Cornfield Ave

Smoketown Rd

Dunker
Church

Visitor Center

walking trails

34

Shepherdstown Pike

Observation
Tower

Richardson
Ave

Sharpsburg Pike

Mondell Rd

65

Antietam Creek

Porterstown Rd

Rodman Ave

Main St

Church St

34 Sharpsburg

Harpers Ferry Rd

Branch Ave

Burnside Bridge Rd

Churchey Rd

Millers Sawmill Rd

Antietam
Driving Tour

0   miles   0.5

Hal Jespersen

Touring the Battlefield

This eight-stop route, which starts at the Visitor Center, will take you to the most notable places at Antietam National Battlefield. From Stop 2 on, it follows the park auto tour, though with different numbers for each stop. The text also offers visitors the chance to see related sites at Harpers Ferry and South Mountain, although those areas do not appear on the tour map.

A 1953 image of the famous Burnside Bridge at Antietam, one of the most noted landmarks of the American Civil War. (nps)

Foreword

BY JOHN D. HOPTAK

Antietam.

It is a Native American word—Algonquian, in its origin—meaning, or so most believe, "swift water" or "swiftly flowing water." It was the name given to a creek, a tributary of the Potomac River, that runs just over forty miles in total length, from its headwaters in south-central Pennsylvania to just a few miles south of the town of Sharpsburg, in western Maryland, where it empties into the Potomac. It was also the name given, at least by soldiers in blue and by the people of the United States, to a horrific battle that was waged near the creek in September 1862.

Undeniably there are few other words in American history that can instantly evoke such solemn emotion and conjure up such sobering sentiment.

Antietam.

The bloodiest single-day battle of the American Civil War.

Antietam.

A hellishly terrible battle fought on the otherwise idyllic and rolling farming fields in western Maryland, near that small town of Sharpsburg, and just to the west of that swiftly-flowing creek.

It is for the casualties that Antietam is still best remembered. On that bloody Wednesday—the seventeenth day of September, 1862—coincidentally

While soldiers fought across many fields of corn during the war, only one became known as *The* Cornfield. (cm)

A statue of Brig. Gen. James Nagle stands atop the monument to the 48th Pennsylvania. A painter and veteran of the Mexican War, Nagle led a brigade in Samuel Sturgis's division at Antietam, taking part in the fight both at Burnside Bridge and in the IX Corps assault on Sharpsburg. (cb)

the 75th anniversary of the signing of the United States Constitution—more than 23,000 soldiers, wearing the uniform of either the United States or of the Confederate States of America, fell dead or wounded or were captured or went listed among the missing. 23,000 casualties, in a fight that lasted but thirteen hours, from just before sunrise to just after sunset. It is difficult—impossible even—to comprehend such carnage in such a short space of time. But it happened—and only, as of the time of this writing, 155 years ago.

Antietam occupies a solemn yet momentous place in the American psyche and in American history. And the now-quiet fields upon which the battle was so earnestly fought must certainly rank among the most pristine of all of America's Civil War battlefields. It is today a beautiful, almost unaltered landscape: quiet, peaceful, reverential. Well-known and instantly recognizable battlefield landmarks such as the stone, three-arched Burnside Bridge and the simple whitewashed square meetinghouse of the Baptist Brethren, stand today as silent witnesses of the awful struggle, while the monuments that today dot the landscape offer up mute testimonials of the bravery, leadership, courage, and sacrifice so widely exhibited upon those very same fields all those years ago.

Yet the significance of this sanguinary struggle extended far beyond the staggering numbers and even well beyond the heroism and bravery so prominently on display. The battle of Antietam brought an end to the Confederate army's first drive north of the Potomac, its first invasion of Union soil in the war's eastern theater. With its victory at Antietam, along with its victory at South Mountain three days prior, the Union army was able to wrestle the initiative from the much-lauded Robert E. Lee and his Army of Northern Virginia and turn back the rising tide of Confederate victories that began three months earlier and more than a 150 miles away to the south.

Just as significant—indeed, even more so—the Union victory at Antietam provided President Abraham Lincoln his long-hoped-for impetus, or basis, for issuing the Emancipation Proclamation, truly one of the most important turning points of the conflict, and in all of American history. At once, the Proclamation struck a blow—a heavy blow—against the social, political, and economic foundation of the Confederate States of America, slavery. And with this, it was made clear, to the people of the warring nations and to the people of the world, that this American Civil War was no longer being fought solely to restore the United States of old, but to create a new nation, a more perfect Union, as it were, to better make good the promises made in the Declaration of Independence.

And Antietam was a victory for the Union. Traditionally, the common interpretation holds that while the campaign resulted in a Union win, the battle itself was a draw, a tie, a tactical stalemate. Traditional interpretation concludes that the battle was waged poorly by the Union brass, in a disjointed manner, with an inept (or cowardly or downright villainous) general—George McClellan—at the helm, and with legions of men in blue held back in reserve, never used. But this is not so.

Nine months after Antietam, Lee drove north again and this time made it farther north, into Pennsylvania. And as was the case during the Maryland (Antietam) campaign, Lee was caught rather off guard by a vigorous Union pursuit and forced to give battle in Pennsylvania on ground not entirely of his own choosing. The result, of course, was a horrific battle, the bloodiest of the war: Gettysburg. As was true after the carnage of Antietam, Lee held his position the day after the combat ended at Gettysburg then deftly maneuvered his army away from the battlefield and slipped safely across the Potomac, leaving Abraham Lincoln greatly frustrated with the general then leading the Army of the Potomac, George Meade. But yet, while the two campaigns ended in much the same way—from a strategic, or strictly military point of view, at least—one would be hard-pressed to hear a historian or a serious student of the conflict refer to Gettysburg as a draw, as a tactical stalemate. It was a U.S. victory, as was Antietam.

True, maybe more could have been done at Antietam—but this question can be applied to almost every other battle of the Civil War, including Gettysburg. And while so much is often made about the ragged, worn-out condition of Lee's soldiers during the campaign—and very rightly so—very seldom do we read or hear of the poor, worn-out condition of the soldiers in blue, or of their morale following their recent, stinging battlefield defeats, or of the fact that one-quarter of the Union soldiers marched into battle for the first time at Antietam.

All too often, we look back, with the full knowledge of how the war ended—and wonder why it did not end sooner. Seldom, though, do we consider the vast pressure resting upon the shoulders of McClellan and of his men in mid-September, 1862. They did not—indeed, could not—know how the war would end. What McClellan did know was that he could not lose in Maryland. Despite this pressure, and despite his belief in the numeric inferiority of his army, McClellan and the Union army were on the offensive. They attacked at South Mountain and attacked again at Antietam. At Antietam, the two sides—Union and Confederate— fought with iron grit and a bitter, fierce stubbornness—the casualties, of course, a testament to the ferocity of the combat. Throughout the day, Union forces attacked and by day's end had everywhere driven back Lee's initial lines of battle, from south of farmer David Miller's cornfield to south of the Dunker Church, more than half a mile away; from out of the Sunken Lane another half a mile or so, to a new line west of the Hagerstown Road; and from along the very banks of the Antietam Creek, at the Burnside Bridge and at the nearby Snavely Ford, to the dominating heights three-quarters-of-a-mile west, just on the southern edge of Sharpsburg. Only the timely arrival of Confederate reinforcements throughout the day— whether they were under John Bell Hood, Lafayette McLaws, or, most famously, A. P. Hill—saved the Army of Northern Virginia from potentially total ruin. The Confederates retreated the following night, leaving the battlefield in Union hands. The war would continue, of course, but with the Emancipation Proclamation, it would continue with a new purpose.

Much has been written about the battle of Antietam, about the campaign, and about its consequences. And much of what has been written recently challenges the traditional interpretation and the common narrative of the battle being a draw, and of it being a disjointed battle fought in three distinct phases. George McClellan's generalship during the campaign and battle has also been reexamined of late in a more fair and more favorable light. *That Field of Blood*, by Daniel Vermilya, reflects and incorporates this most recent scholarship and offers, as he writes in his introduction, a "fresh narrative" in an effort, he states, "to move past outdated myths on the campaign." This book, as are all the others in the Emerging Civil War series, is intended to be a clear, concise introduction to the battle, best suited for and directed toward those who are perhaps visiting the battlefield of Antietam for the first time and who are seeking not only a summary of the action and the significance of the battle, but also an easy-to-follow guide for touring the battlefield. This short work, lavishly illustrated and easy to follow, helps to make sense of the awful carnage and of the confused, chaotic fighting. It well summarizes the campaign and its legacies, and it provides a fine step-by-step guide for touring what is today one of America's most pristine Civil War battlefields.

JOHN HOPTAK *is the author of* THE BATTLE OF SOUTH MOUNTAIN *and* CONFRONTATION AT GETTYSBURG, *among other works. He worked for a number of years as a park ranger at Antietam National Battlefield and is currently employed at Gettysburg National Military Park.*

"Upon this field of Antietam was fought one of the most desperate battles of the War of the Rebellion, upon the outcome of which hung the destinies and liberties of millions of human beings."

– Robert P. Kennedy
23rd Ohio Volunteer Infantry
dedication of Ohio monuments at Antietam
October 13, 1903

THE
PHILADELPHIA BRIGADE
ORGANIZATION
SIXTY-NINTH
SEVENTY-FIRST
SEVENTY-SECOND
ONE HUNDRED AND SIXTH
REGIMENTS OF
PENNSYLVANIA INFANTRY

SECOND CORPS

PROLOGUE

When the Civil War began, Elwood Rodebaugh was a shoemaker in the small town of Canton, Pennsylvania. He had neither wealth nor fame. Had the Civil War not erupted over issues of slavery, freedom, and the future expansion of the nation, his name likely would have never made it into any history books. We don't know what Elwood's politics were, or what he thought of the causes of the war. He was, in every way, a common citizen.

Elwood was 31 years old when the first shots of the war were fired. His wife, Josephine, was 26. The couple was married July 3, 1856, and had two young children. Charles was two years old, and Heloise was not quite four in April 1861. The family had a few milk cows and a small home near Canton, miles away from the turmoil that was spreading through the nation.

On August 26, 1861, Elwood found himself caught up in the great conflagration of war. He left his family and enlisted as a private in the 106th Pennsylvania. We know nothing of his reasons for joining, only that he volunteered to serve his country in its hour of need.

As a member of the 106th, Elwood's Civil War journey took him south into Virginia. His regiment was involved in the actions around Ball's Bluff in

The 106th Pennsylvania is among the units listed on the Philadelphia Brigade monument in Antietam's West Woods. (cm)

October 1861. The following summer, on June 29, 1862, he was wounded in the forearm at the battle of Savage Station—part of the Seven Days' Battles outside of Richmond—though he stayed on the field for the duration of the fight. Despite his wound, he remained with the regiment as it was recalled to Washington when the Peninsula campaign came to an end. In early September 1862, he marched north onto the dusty roads of Maryland, filing along with the Army of the Potomac as Union forces pursued gray- and butternut-clad Southerners toward the town of Sharpsburg, along the banks of Antietam Creek. There, Elwood was one of nearly 100,000 soldiers caught up in the bloodiest day in American history on September 17, 1862.

Antietam was the first battlefield ever to be photographed before the dead were buried. Images such as this one—showing the lone grave of Pvt. John Marshall, Company L, 28th Pennsylvania—haunted those who had never seen the impact of war. These historic photographs were taken by Alexander Gardner and his assistant James Gibson several days after the battle. (loc)

At the battle of Antietam, in the span of just 12 hours, more than 23,000 men were killed, wounded, or missing in action. Never before, and never since, has the country seen a day of such slaughter. On the morning of the battle, Elwood and the 106th Pennsylvania found themselves fighting in Antietam's West Woods. As a ferocious Confederate attack swept into their ranks, the men of the 106th were overwhelmed by the enemy and driven from the field. According to Capt. William Jones, his company commander, Elwood "was last seen, when we commenced falling back, fighting bravely."

In the aftermath of the fight, it was not until Friday, September 19, that Federal troops again regained the West Woods. By then, two days of September sunshine had made the field of dead bodies a terrible sight. The dead were buried—both the known and those whose names were unknown. The burial crews did not see Elwood among the dead, and he was simply listed as missing in action. While the official roster listed him missing, those who had fought with Elwood knew what had happened: he had been killed in action.

In 1863, Josephine Rodebaugh applied for a widow's pension to care for her two young children. According to the pension documents, she could neither read nor write, as she simply made her mark with an "x." A letter was submitted on her behalf from Samuel Riggs and Daniel Fitzwater, both members of Company D. Riggs and Fitzwater each stated that Elwood had been killed in battle, but because he had shaved off his heavy beard just days before the fight, burial parties did not recognize his remains. As a result, he was buried as an unknown soldier. Captain Jones wrote two letters confirming this account, adding that each time Elwood went into combat, he did so "with unflinching bravery."

The peaceful waters of Antietam Creek, taken in September 1862. (loc)

With these letters as evidence of her husband's sacrifice, Josephine received her widow's pension. She later remarried, only to lose her second husband to death as well. Josephine lived on with Elwood's memory until her own death on May 6, 1905. Elwood's children, Heloise and Charles, grew up never knowing their father.

Elwood's story, and indeed, the story of his family, is but one of thousands that were forever changed by Antietam. Though he died at Antietam and was buried as an unknown soldier, Elwood's story didn't end in Sharpsburg, Maryland, in September 1862. The legacies of those who died in that battle live on in the history their sacrifices made.

*   *   *

When I was young, I learned of Antietam and its importance in a very personal way. Elwood was my great-great-great grandfather, and his story was passed down to me from my own father and grandfather. I remember being given an old regimental history of the 106th Pennsylvania, and seeing the words "killed at Antietam" next to

Elwood's name in the regimental roster. When I was nine years old, my parents took me on my first visit to Antietam National Battlefield so I could walk the same fields my ancestor had walked over 125 years earlier. I will never forget that first visit to Antietam.

Here, the history of the United States had forever changed. This was the battle that turned the tide of the Civil War, a Union victory at a time when one was sorely needed by the North. This was the battle that led to the Emancipation Proclamation. This was the battle that saw more casualties in one day than any other in American history. And it was ordinary people—simple shoemakers, fathers, and husbands—who were the ones who gave this battle its extraordinary importance.

Alexander Gardner took this photo of Col. Turner Morehead, 106th Pennsylvania, on the battlefield in the aftermath of the fighting. Morehead was the commander of the 106th Pennsylvania, the author's great-great-great grandfather Elwood Rodebaugh's regiment. (loc)

The title of this book, *That Field of Blood*, is drawn from the writings of Reverend William Wallace Lyle, the Scottish-born chaplain of the 11th Ohio. Lyle published his wartime reminiscences, *Lights and Shadows of Army Life*, in 1865, and his passages on the aftermath of Antietam show the true human cost of the battle. Lyle did what he could to help in his regiment's field hospital in the days following the fight, and for every soldier he saw who was maimed or killed in battle, Lyle thought of the loved ones at home as well, "far from that field of blood."

For those who have been visiting Antietam for years and have studied the minutiae of the battle, this book will not delve deeply into the details of Antietam. It is not meant to be an exhaustive study. Many other volumes are devoted to the strategic and tactical intricacies of the battle, written by historians for whom I have an incredible amount of respect. A list of them can be found in this book's accompanying bibliography, which is posted online, and also in the Suggested Reading section at the back.

That Field of Blood is meant, rather, to be a guide and introduction for those looking to learn of Antietam and its significance in American history. By providing a fresh narrative and overview of the battle—using recent scholarship to move past outdated myths on the campaign—I hope that veteran history buffs and first-time battlefield visitors alike can all find something worthwhile in these pages. Much like the other works in the Emerging Civil War series, this book is intended as a

This image of dead Confederate soldiers in front of the Dunker Church is among the most iconic shots of the American Civil War. These men were likely part of Col. S. D. Lee's Artillery Battalion. (loc)

guide, with driving directions to various stops, as well as specific vignettes and things to look for around Antietam National Battlefield. The driving stops here are meant to be a starting point, and they do not all align with the NPS driving tour of the battlefield. You are also encouraged to explore the battlefield through its many trails, and to see the monuments and War Department tablets, for they help to tell Antietam's fascinating story as well. This book can also be read away from the field as an overview of the battle.

In writing this book, it was my goal to convey the significance of Antietam to those who hope to walk the fields where Elwood Rodebaugh and thousands of others fell in battle in September 1862. Perhaps more than any other battle,

Antietam changed the nature of the Civil War itself. By studying the battle today, we can honor the legacies of those who struggled on "that field of blood" more than 150 years ago.

This lone Confederate soldier killed at Antietam was just one of more than 23,000 casualties who fell on September 17, 1862. (loc)

"The Most Propitious Time"

CHAPTER ONE

SUMMER OF 1862

The Antietam campaign played out over the course of two and a half weeks in September 1862. Its seeds were planted several months earlier and more than 150 miles south of the quiet town of Sharpsburg, Maryland, where the campaign would eventually witness its bloody and savage apogee. In the spring of 1862, the grand Union Army of the Potomac, built by the enigmatic Maj. Gen. George Brinton McClellan, launched a massive campaign to capture the Confederate capital of Richmond. After months of preparing and amidst the pressures of Washington, McClellan sailed his army down the Virginia coast, then landed and advanced on Richmond from the east to seize the rebel capital in one fell swoop. Confederate forces under the command of Gen. Joseph Johnston positioned themselves to block McClellan's advance, only to methodically retreat over the course of several weeks. By the end of May, McClellan's army was within a day's march of the Confederate capital.

While the situation appeared dire for the nascent Confederacy, a dramatic change occurred on the doorstep of Richmond. During the battle of Seven Pines, Joseph Johnston was wounded and rendered unable to command his army. In his place, Gen. Robert E. Lee took command of Richmond's defenders,

Because of its status as a Border State, the Maryland Monument is the only one on the field representing troops from both sides. There were both Union and Confederate soldiers from Maryland who fought at Antietam. The monument was dedicated on May 30, 1900. President William McKinley spoke at its dedication. The Dunker Church sits in the background. (cb)

beginning his remarkable tenure as the commander of the Army of Northern Virginia.

Over the next month, Lee strengthened his position and prepared to reclaim the Virginia Peninsula. Lee launched a bold counteroffensive in late June that

led to the Seven Days' Battles which, despite tactical setbacks at several of the engagements, ultimately forced McClellan and his army to fall back to the James River, swinging the momentum and strategic advantage back to the Confederacy.

Over the coming weeks, the war had different courses in store for both Lee and

This view looks east from the Antietam Visitor Center across the battlefield at Antietam. South Mountain can be seen seven miles in the distance. (cb)

McClellan. The Union commander, nicknamed the "Young Napoleon," was recalled to Washington along with his army, large portions of which were siphoned off and given to Maj. Gen. John Pope and his Army of Virginia. Promising no quarter to the enemy, Pope was the stark opposite of the often cautious McClellan, which was exactly why the Lincoln administration favored Pope's approach to the war.

Lee found his new opponent bombastic and foolish. Accordingly, he made John Pope and his army pay. Lee's trusted subordinate, Maj. Gen. Thomas Jonathan "Stonewall" Jackson, engaged part of Pope's army at Cedar Mountain on August 9, achieving a stunning victory.

A bell from the aircraft carrier the USS *Antietam* sits on permanent loan from the American Legion next to the visitor center parking lot. The ship, which weighed more than 27,000 tons and stretched more than 880 feet long, served from 1945-1963. (cm)

In the coming weeks, Jackson moved north, threatening Pope's supply base and his connection with Washington. By late August, the two sides had arrived at the same battlefield where the battle of First Manassas had been fought just over one year earlier. On the evening of August 28, a new battle began. The violence spilled into the following two days, making the Second Battle of Manassas one of the bloodiest engagements of the Civil War. By the end of the day on August 30, Union forces were once again retreating from Manassas, and Pope had been vanquished. Within just 90 days, Lee had successfully taken the war from the gates of Richmond to the gates of Washington.

Lee did not take such stunning success lightly, for he had even greater goals in mind.

* * *

It is fitting that the Maryland campaign was begun by a man such as Lee, whose character and foundation were rooted deeply in American history. Born to a prestigious Virginia family, Lee was among the most highly sought after officers on either side when the Civil War began. A graduate of the West Point Class of 1829, Lee built an exemplary service record as an engineer. He performed admirably and bravely in the Mexican War, serving on the staff of Winfield Scott. Accordingly, at the outset of the Civil War, Lee was offered a command in the Union army, only to turn it down, resign from the U.S. Army, and become a Confederate general. After a command in western Virginia and serving as a military advisor to Confederate President Jefferson Davis, Lee took field command of the Army of Northern Virginia in June 1862, and he held it through the rest of the war. Lee was bold and audacious, garnering the respect of generals and privates alike. It was these characteristics that were on full display in September 1862.

With his success at Second Manassas in mind, Lee was thinking in bold strategic terms as August gave way to September. On September 3, while encamped near Leesburg, Virginia, Lee laid out his thoughts on what lay ahead in a letter to Jefferson Davis. "The present seems to be the most propitious time since the commencement of the war for the Confederate Army to enter Maryland," Lee began. Federal forces in Washington had suffered

Nearly one of every four Union soldiers at Antietam was from the state of New York. To honor them, New York dedicated this monument on September 17, 1920. The monument stands roughly 58 feet high, and it is seen here looking east, with South Mountain in the distance. (cb)

This is a close-up view of the bronze plaque on the New York Monument. (cb)

The Dunker Church, one of Antietam's most famous landmarks, sits along the historic Hagerstown Pike and saw soldiers of both sides move past it during the battle. (cb)

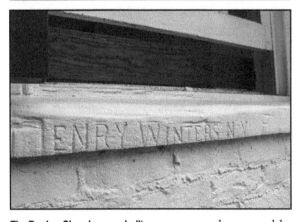

The Dunker Church was rebuilt in 1962 using many original materials, including pieces that veterans had carved their names into upon returning to Antietam years later, such as this windowsill. (cb)

greatly in recent defeats, and though Lee's army was weakened as well, he knew it would be wise to strike before any reinforcements could arrive. "[W]e cannot afford to be idle," he reasoned. Though his army was smaller than the Federal force defending Washington, Lee still believed it necessary "to harass if we cannot destroy them. I am aware that the movement is attended with much risk, yet I do not consider success impossible, and shall endeavor to guard it from loss."

Following Second Manassas, Lee knew the longer he waited to start a new campaign, the stronger Union armies would become. Moreover, Lee also knew that the longer the war went on, Northern states would have a greater ability to bring their advantages in strength and industry to bear on the South. Thus, it was time for a new strategy. It was time to take the war into Maryland, a crucial border state that many Southerners desired to see become part of the Confederacy.

While it was unlikely that Maryland would actually secede and join the South, a Confederate presence there would put considerable pressure on the Lincoln administration and Union troops in Washington to act. Indeed, Lee's goal was to move into Maryland, draw Union forces out away from the capital, and defeat them in battle. A campaign in Maryland would grant Virginia a reprieve from being the seat of war, taking the war to the people of the North, as well.

On a larger scale, events elsewhere beckoned larger strategic consequences for a Confederate movement into Maryland. Farther west, Confederates under Braxton Bragg had begun a campaign northward toward Kentucky, and across the Atlantic, England and France were anxiously watching events in Virginia and elsewhere to determine if it was time to officially recognize the Confederacy as a separate and independent nation. A Confederate victory in Maryland could have profound consequences extending far beyond the state, signaling to the world that the Confederacy was ready for its independence.

Having explained his thinking to Jefferson Davis, Lee did not wait long. The following day he issued orders that in effect began the Maryland campaign. With the Confederate army near Leesburg, the Potomac River was not far. On September 4, Maj. Gen. Daniel Harvey Hill's division crossed the Potomac. The rest of the army followed over the next two days; Jackson's men crossed on the 5th, and Maj. Gen. James Longstreet's command on the 6th. During the Maryland campaign, the Army of Northern Virginia was operating in a loosely organized wing command structure, with nine infantry divisions divided between Lee's top two generals, Stonewall Jackson and James Longstreet.

By deciding to enter Union territory for the first time, Lee was taking a bold risk. Lee knew his men were tired and worn from recent battles, though he likely did not realize how exhausted they had actually become. While he loathed the idea of embarking on a lengthy campaign, he knew a moment of golden opportunity had arrived. It was time to seek a greater reward by hazarding a campaign into Maryland. In moving north, Lee hoped to potentially end the war with one bold move. His army could be cut off and destroyed, or they could deliver a death blow to the country they had once called their own.

By the end of the day on September 6, Confederate forces were arriving in Frederick, and the Maryland campaign was underway.

* * *

While Lee and the Confederates were on the move, major changes were occurring in

Robert E. Lee began his career as an officer in the United States Army. (loc)

By September 1862, Robert E. Lee had moved the front line of the war from the gates of Richmond to north of the Potomac River. (loc)

Washington. Only a few weeks before, Lincoln had ordered George McClellan back from the Virginia Peninsula, ending the Young Napoleon's grand campaign in failure. Now, with thousands of soldiers streaming back into the defenses of Washington, Lincoln needed a commander to rebuild the army. The president was faced with the daunting decision of placing McClellan

back in command, an action that was rife with controversy because of the mutual disdain that existed between the general and the Lincoln administration.

A student at the University of Pennsylvania at age 13 and a West Point cadet at age 15, George McClellan was well educated and rose quickly in life. During the Mexican War, he served on the staff of Winfield Scott. In the 1850s, McClellan worked as an army engineer, training cadets at West Point and working on various fortifications before leaving the army to become a railroad executive.

This modern-day view shows the location of Gardner's famous image of the dead in front of the Dunker Church. (cb)

When the Civil War began, McClellan's services were in high demand. McClellan had early success commanding troops in western Virginia, and after the disastrous Union defeat at First Manassas, he was called to Washington to take command of the troops in the capital. By November, he was made general in chief of the army, a position he would not hold for long.

After several months in Washington preparing for a new campaign, Lincoln's patience with McClellan grew thin. He was removed as general in chief upon embarking for the Peninsula campaign, which, despite its early promise, ultimately ended in failure. After months of bickering and disagreements between him and the Lincoln administration, when McClellan was recalled to Washington, it appeared as though his time as a commander was at an end.

Maj. Gen. George B. McClellan wrote candid letters to his wife, Mary Ellen, that provide fascinating insight into his enigmatic personality. (loc)

And yet, in early September, Lincoln turned to McClellan once again to reorganize Union troops

The foundation of the original Dunker Church, pictured in 1953. Nine years after this picture was taken, the church was rebuilt on this original foundation, using many of the original materials. (nps)

following the defeat at Manassas. On September 2, McClellan was officially given command of all Union forces in the capital, including his old Army of the Potomac and John Pope's defeated Army of Virginia.

Lincoln did not turn to McClellan out of personal fondness for him. The two men did not see eye to eye on much, including the strategic goals of the war. McClellan had a staunchly conservative view of the war, opposing any radical social or political changes that the conflict might bring. Lincoln was, at that time, contemplating presidential action against slavery in the form of an emancipation proclamation, one that would forever change the country.

By turning to McClellan, Lincoln was acknowledging the dire situation facing the nation. Union forces were in no condition to fight, and Lee's victorious Army of Northern Virginia was just over 30 miles away from the capital.

In short, Lincoln needed a general to rebuild the army, and he needed one who could do it in less than a week. McClellan was the man for the job. Indeed, McClellan himself wrote, just after receiving command once again, "this week is the crisis of our fate."

While McClellan's reputation as a battlefield commander is not held in high regard among many historians today, his work in reassembling the Army of the Potomac from its shattered remnants in early September was nothing short of extraordinary. With little time to waste,

An artillery display outside the visitor center showcases four of the most common types of cannon used on the battlefield: 10-pounder Parrott, 3-inch ordnance rifle, a model 1857 12-pounder Napoleon, and a model 1841 6-pounder smoothbore. (cm)

McClellan quickly sorted through the various commands in Washington, determining which were fit to fight and which needed to rest and refit. In the span of five days, McClellan engineered a new army. It was assembled from remnants of McClellan's old Army of the Potomac from the Peninsula, pieces of John Pope's Army of Virginia from the Second Manassas campaign, plus four other separate army divisions that were built into the new IX Corps. Disease and casualties had thinned the ranks, and the officer corps suffered from major lapses in experience and cohesion. The army was far from an unstoppable fighting machine, but it would have to do.

Within days of being given his new command, McClellan was on the move. On September 7, he moved his headquarters out of Washington and into Maryland, signaling the start of a new campaign.

At the Visitor Center

Antietam National Battlefield is one of the best-preserved Civil War battlefields in the country. The park features a driving tour, as well as numerous trails for exploring parts of the battlefield in greater depth.

The visitor center's observation deck offers a panoramic view of the battlefield. (cm)

Inside the Antietam Visitor Center, the park runs an orientation film throughout the day. Museum exhibits also help to tell the story of Antietam. Make sure to visit the observation room to get a panoramic view of the northern two-thirds of the battlefield.

Before leaving the visitor center, take some time to walk around the building and see some of the monuments. A paved walkway facilitates this short walking tour. The New York State Monument, Maryland Monument, 20th New York Monument, and guns representing part of Col. S. D. Lee's Artillery Battalion are all easily accessible.

Just across the road from the visitor center is the famed Dunker Church. Take a few moments to walk over and explore this historic Civil War landmark before departing on the tour. Originally built in 1852, the church survived the battle, only to be blown down during a storm in the 1920s. Using some of the original materials, the church was rebuilt in 1962 for the centennial anniversary of Antietam. The Dunkers who worshipped there were German Baptist Brethren. They were also pacifists.

Antietam National Battlefield sees an average of about 375,000 visitors a year, although more than half a million visited during the Civil War Sesquicentennial. (cm)

GPS: N 39.47381 W 77.74499

The Campaign Begins

CHAPTER TWO

SEPTEMBER 7-15, 1862

With Union forces now on the move, the campaign was in full swing. By September 7, Lee and his army had gathered in Frederick, though they would not stay there for long. When he first came into Maryland, Lee did so under the assumption that a Union garrison at Harpers Ferry—more than 20 miles away from Frederick—would be driven away by the Confederate presence. Sitting at the northern end of the Shenandoah Valley, and at the confluence of the Potomac and Shenandoah Rivers, Harpers Ferry was crucial for both sides during the Civil War. Lee needed it clear of Federal forces for his campaign to ensure lines of supply and communication running south into Virginia. Thus, when Union forces held their position, a major problem emerged for Lee—one that threatened to derail his campaign.

On September 9, Lee issued Special Orders 191, splitting his army into several pieces in order to address this problem. The largest contingent of Lee's forces was sent to the west toward Harpers Ferry and Martinsburg, where Col. Dixon Miles and Brig. Gen. Julius White respectively held their garrisons. This force consisted of the divisions of Maj. Gen. Lafayette McLaws and Brig. Gen. John Walker, as well as the command of Stonewall Jackson. The rest of the Confederate army was split between

One of the off-the-beaten-path sites of the Maryland campaign, the North Carolina Monument at Fox's Gap, is along a short trail that stretches from a nearby parking area. Placed there in 2003, the monument marks where Confederates tried to stave off Federal attacks throughout the day on September 14, 1862 during the battle of South Mountain. (dv)

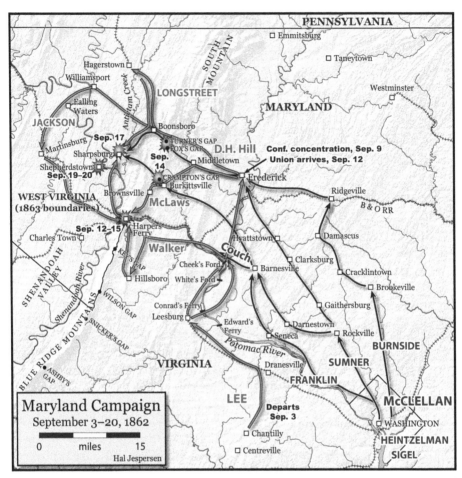

MARYLAND CAMPAIGN, SEPTEMBER 3-20, 1862—The campaign began when Robert E. Lee's Army of Northern Virginia crossed into Maryland in early September, heading first to Frederick before dividing and heading west toward Hagerstown, Martinsburg, and Harpers Ferry. Because Lee divided his army, Union forces were able to catch up with the Confederates, bringing them to battle first at South Mountain, several days before the eventual climactic fight at Antietam on September 17.

South Mountain, where D. H. Hill positioned his division, and the city of Hagerstown, where the rest of Longstreet's command was initially sent. According to Lee's orders, the forces were to have reached their goals in three days—on Friday, September 12—enough time for the Confederates to regather, turn, and await the approach of the Army of the Potomac from Washington.

Just as coming into Maryland was a risk, Lee gambled once again with Special Orders 191. He trusted his men and their leaders, believing they could drive out the nearby Union garrisons before

Maj. Gen. Thomas J. "Stonewall" Jackson had spent time commanding a garrison at Harpers Ferry at the very beginning of the war, so he knew well the town's strengths and weaknesses. (loc)

Maj. Gen. James Longstreet was one of Lee's two wing commanders in the Maryland campaign. The other was Stonewall Jackson. (loc)

Federal troops could catch up with the divided Confederates in Maryland.

Unfortunately for Lee, the Confederate columns did not reach Harpers Ferry as quickly as he had hoped. When Jackson's approach caused White's men to flee Martinsburg, he turned his focus on Harpers Ferry. He arrived there on September 12 only to find that the Confederates had not yet seized the high ground around the town. Now, with Jackson in charge, the Confederates went about taking the surrounding heights, trapping Union troops below. Although delayed, the Confederates were coiling their grip around the Union garrison.

Time, however, was not on the side of the Confederates. Late in the day on September 12, just as the last vestiges of the Army of Northern Virginia were leaving Frederick, advance elements of the Army of the Potomac began to arrive. The following day, when the Union XII Corps arrived in town, several soldiers from the 27th Indiana came across an envelope with a copy of Lee's Special Orders 191 and two cigars enclosed. Upon realizing the importance

A Civil War Trails marker at the Best farm on Monocacy National Battlefield tells the story of Lee's "lost order," which has subsequently generated some of the biggest "what ifs" of the Civil War. (cm)

of their find, the papers were passed up through the chain of command, eventually arriving at McClellan's headquarters.

While this has long been hailed as one of the great intelligence coups of the war, the reality of the find did not quite match the hype that it would later generate. What McClellan had in his hands on the 13th was a copy of Lee's orders from September 9. They were four days old and referred to goals that were supposed to have been met on Friday the 12th. Thus, there was no way of knowing precisely how accurate they still were. They also said nothing of Confederate strength. What the orders did tell McClellan, however, was that the Confederate army was divided in an attempt to capture Harpers Ferry and continue its drive north.

The battle of South Mountain on September 14, 1862, was a key turning point in the Maryland campaign. While it is often overlooked today, South Mountain saw greater combined casualties than the battle of First Manassas. (loc)

After sending out cavalry to verify the information contained in the orders, McClellan decided his best course of action would be to strike against the Confederate forces closest, those on South Mountain. As McClellan himself noted, he intended to "cut the enemy in two and beat him in detail." By 6:00 p.m., he issued orders for the following day.

*   *   *

Maj. Gen. Jesse Reno, commander of the Union IX Corps, was killed at South Mountain. (loc)

Although dramatically overshadowed today by the events of Antietam just three days later, the battle of South Mountain on September 14 was a crucial event for the Maryland campaign. Indeed, without South Mountain, Antietam would not have occurred as it did, or even at all.

The plan that McClellan issued on September 13 called for the Union army to push through three separate gaps in South Mountain, offering the possibility of breaking Confederate resistance there and liberating the beleaguered garrison at Harpers Ferry.

On the Union right, the I Corps, commanded by the recently promoted Maj. Gen. Joseph Hooker, was to advance against Frosttown and Turner's Gaps, pressing the Confederate left. Just one mile south of Turner's Gap, Maj. Gen. Jesse Reno's IX Corps was to take Fox's Gap. Several miles south of there, Maj. Gen. William Franklin had the task of seizing Crampton's Gap, upon which Franklin's VI Corps was to then push through to the west into Pleasant Valley, applying pressure to the rear of the Confederate position at Maryland Heights overlooking Harpers Ferry and possibly relieving the Union garrison there.

Alfred Waud sketched soldiers marching through Middletown, Maryland, during the Maryland campaign. (loc)

Throughout the day, combat raged off and on at the gaps in the mountain. Casualties quickly mounted on each side. Confederate reinforcements were rushed up to the mountain as Lee desperately tried to stave off the Federal attack. By nightfall, Union forces had made significant gains, although they had not quite achieved the victory that McClellan had sought.

That evening, Lee knew that his campaign was in grave danger. His army was divided and greatly outnumbered, and the Federals were poised to push through the mountain passes for good the following morning. At 8:00 p.m., Lee sent out orders for his army to begin a retreat from Maryland back into Virginia. While Lee was willing to take significant risks, he was not willing to face the likelihood that his army could be torn apart while it remained divided on Maryland soil. Thus, the wiser option was to fall back to Virginia, regroup, and then reevaluate his options. Lee directed Jackson's men to disengage from Harpers Ferry and move to Shepherdstown, where the rest of the army would soon cross the Potomac.

Brig. Gen. Alfred Pleasonton commanded McClellan's cavalry division in the Maryland campaign. (loc)

On the morning of the 15th, Lee's retreat was underway.

As Lee's men headed west along the Boonsboro Turnpike, marching toward the Potomac River, their commander was hoping for word from Harpers Ferry before leaving Maryland altogether. He knew that part of his forces there, the division of Lafayette McLaws, was still on the Maryland side of the river on Maryland Heights, and could potentially be cut off from the rest of the army. To protect McLaws's flank, Lee decided to wait before crossing the Potomac.

A row of artillery pieces marks the Federal position on Bolivar Heights, one of the many ridgelines held by Col. Dixon Miles's command at Harpers Ferry in September 1862. (cm)

He moved his command to the town of Sharpsburg, which offered better terrain for staging a possible defense. Furthermore, having risked so much thus far, Lee was reluctant to withdraw from Maryland entirely, and was hoping good news from Harpers Ferry might salvage the campaign.

By noon, Lee and his columns from South Mountain had arrived around Sharpsburg and had begun setting up defensive lines. It was then that Lee finally received word from Jackson at Harpers Ferry, a message with news he had been so desperately awaiting. "Through God's blessing Harper's Ferry and its garrison are to be surrendered," Jackson proclaimed. While the surrender occurred several days later than Lee had wanted, it was still a success for the Confederates, helping to offset the defeat at South Mountain. Soon, Jackson's men in Harpers Ferry would be free to reunite with Lee and the main body of the army.

Confederate general Samuel Garland was killed at South Mountain, September 14, 1862. (loc)

While Lee was not yet fully intent on making a stand at Sharpsburg, hoping to first reunite his army, Jackson's message had managed to breathe new life into Lee's campaign. The capture of Harpers Ferry would stand as one of the great successes of Jackson's illustrious Civil War career, and it was the largest surrender of United States soldiers up until the fall of the Philippines in World War II. More than 12,000 Federals had fallen into Confederate hands. And yet, as gratifying as this success was, the most important part of it—for Robert E. Lee, at least—was that the Army of Northern Virginia could soon be reunited in time to face George McClellan's Army of the Potomac in battle.

Lee had come into Maryland to fight a battle with his army on his terms, and now he might finally have his chance.

At South Mountain and Harpers Ferry

The events discussed in this chapter cover considerable ground in western Maryland. The **South Mountain State Battlefield** consists of the main gaps where fighting occurred on September 14, 1862. You will find GPS coordinates for each stop below. At Turner's Gap, several iron War Department tablets sit alongside Alt. Route 40 and the Appalachian Trail. They

The visitor center at Washington Monument State Park (cm)

are located across from the Old South Mountain Inn. The tablets and the inn are 1.3 miles south of the Washington Monument State Park, where a South Mountain State Battlefield office is located.

GPS: N 39.48480 W 77.62024

Jesse Reno monument (cm)

At **Fox's Gap**, visitors will see several monuments memorializing the fighting. There is a state marker to the 17th Michigan, as well as monuments for Union Maj. Gen. Jesse Reno and Confederate Brig. Gen. Samuel Garland, each of whom died in the fighting there. There is a short trail of about one-quarter mile that leads back to a North Carolina State Monument as well.

GPS: N 39.47061 W 77.61759

War Correspondents memorial (cm)

Six miles south, at **Crampton's Gap**, there are several War Department tablets, as well as a War Correspondent Memorial Arch at Gathland State Park. In addition to the fighting here in 1862, this was the postwar home of George Alfred Townsend, a Civil War journalist. Townsend built the Arch in 1896 to memorialize 157 correspondents from the Civil War.

GPS: N 39.40614 W 77.63919

Harpers Ferry (cm)

You are also encouraged to visit **Harpers Ferry National Historical Park**, which has its own rich history, covering the antebellum U.S. Armory, John Brown's historic 1859 raid, as well as the fascinating story of Storer College. There is a fee for visiting Harpers Ferry, and the best place to begin your visit is at the visitor center on Cavalier Heights. The park includes the 1862 battle grounds around Harpers Ferry, including School House Ridge, Bolivar Heights, Loudon Heights, and Maryland Heights.

GPS: N 39.31603 W 77.75639

▶ To Stop 1

From the visitor center parking lot, head toward the southern driveway (with the visitor center on your left) and proceed 0.1 miles to state route 65. Turn left. Take the first left on Richardson Avenue, about 0.1 miles, being aware of oncoming traffic. Follow Richardson Avenue 1.1 miles, then turn left onto state route 34 East (this will take you across Antietam Creek). In 1.6 miles, turn left at the Pry House (look for the brown NPS sign). Follow the driveway (.2 miles) to the house. The parking lot is on the right near the historic barn.

GPS: N 39.47605 W 77.71328

Samuel Garland monument at Fox's Gap (cm)

McClellan Prepares for Battle

CHAPTER THREE

SEPTEMBER 16, 1862

Having been pushed around repeatedly by Lee's army that summer, the Army of the Potomac had finally notched a victory of its own on the slopes of South Mountain on September 14. McClellan wasted little time sending word of the success to Washington, claiming a "glorious victory." Lincoln was no doubt encouraged by this news, responding with one of the most quoted messages of the entire Maryland campaign: "Your dispatches of today received. God bless you, and all with you. Destroy the rebel army, if possible."

While McClellan's men had cause for optimism, the campaign was far from over. McClellan knew nothing of Lee's decision to withdraw back toward Virginia, and on the morning of the 15th, his army began the process of crossing through the mountain passes they had secured the day before.

While there was some delay that morning, within a few hours, advance elements of the Army of the Potomac descended from South Mountain and entered the town of Boonsboro. The Union columns turned down the Boonsboro Turnpike and began heading west toward Keedysville, following the same route Lee's army had taken just hours before. By that afternoon, Maj. Gen. Israel Richardson's division of the II Corps reached the

The home of Philip and Elizabeth Pry in 1862, George McClellan spent the night of September 16th in this building. For decades, historians believed McClellan made his headquarters here during the battle, but a 2016 *Civil War Times* article by historian Tom Clemens argued that McClellan actually made his headquarters back in Keedysville. Today, the building houses a satellite of the National Museum of Civil War Medicine that focuses on work done by field hospitals. (cm) eastern banks of Antietam Creek. Across the waters, on the high ground rising immediately west of the creek, the Federals saw Lee's men taking position on the high ground around Sharpsburg.

George McClellan arrived near the front around 5:00 p.m., with the rest of his army still making its way westward. By that time, it was too late in the day for any offensive operations, meaning that McClellan would have to wait until the 16th, when more of his army would be available, to determine his next steps.

Sharpsburg today (above) doesn't look quite like it did in 1862 (top), but the town has managed to fend off a lot of the modern commercialization that has spoiled so many other battlefields. (loc)(cm)

*   *   *

As dawn broke on September 16, George McClellan was at Union headquarters in Keedysville, where he wrote a quick message to his wife: "Have reached thus far and have no doubt delivered Penna. and Maryland. Am well and in excellent spirits." While McClellan's message contained an element of truth— his actions at South Mountain had severely damaged Lee's campaign in Maryland, perhaps beyond repair—thousands of Confederates were still on Maryland soil, and they were setting up defensive positions just a few miles to his front around Sharpsburg. There was more work to be done.

The question of what exactly that was remained unanswered, though, due largely to the weather conditions that morning. "This morning a heavy fog has thus far prevented us doing more than to ascertain that some of the enemy are still there," McClellan informed General-in-Chief Henry Halleck. "Do not know in what force. Will attack as soon as situation of enemy is developed."

As McClellan peered into the fog that morning, there were many unknowns regarding Lee's army. While he knew that the Confederates had been divided, he did not know how many troops were in each part of the Confederate forces, especially the part to his front at Sharpsburg. During the campaign, McClellan had received estimates placing Confederate strength anywhere from 80,000 men to more than 200,000. While McClellan did not know how many troops Lee had at Sharpsburg on the 16th, or that the bulk of the reinforcements from Harpers Ferry had not yet arrived, he certainly did not think Lee would risk fighting a battle with only a small portion of his army. Moreover, in the event Confederates still occupied Harpers Ferry, McClellan had to be wary of enemy forces moving north from that area through Pleasant Valley, for they could easily get behind the unsuspecting Union army.

Sharpsburg's Lutheran church.
(loc)

As truth would have it, McClellan's main mistake on September 16 was miscalculating Lee's strategic decision making. McClellan had no idea how strongly Lee wanted his Maryland battle—so much so that Lee would risk fighting with only half of his army as the Federals gathered across the creek. Had the weather not been a problem and had McClellan known the state of Lee's army, perhaps he would have pressed his advantage on the 16th and rushed an attack across the creek and into Confederate lines. Perhaps he could have caught the Confederates off guard and outnumbered, crushing their ranks and dispersing them once and for all.

Fortunately for Lee, and unfortunately for McClellan, that is not what happened. McClellan was faced with a very real strategic situation, and he acted based on his knowledge and assumptions at the time.

As the fog lifted, McClellan's strategy came into focus. First and foremost, he knew he needed to move his forces across the Antietam in a strategic manner. There were three bridges over the creek that would prove beneficial to him. The primary crossing point was known as the Middle Bridge, which carried the Boonsboro Turnpike over the creek. To the south

This Alfred Waud sketch shows citizens fleeing Sharpsburg. (loc)

was the Rohrbach Bridge, known also as the Lower Bridge, and soon to be known to history as Burnside Bridge. To the north was the Upper Bridge, which was also known as the Hitt Bridge. There were few places to ford the creek, making these bridges, and the known fording points, crucial to Union success in the upcoming battle.

McClellan based his battle plan on utilizing the commands positioned on his right and left. He began by ordering Maj. Gen. Joseph Hooker and his I Corps across the Antietam at the site of the Upper Bridge. Hooker was to advance and test Lee's left flank. If Confederates were found in sufficient strength to repulse him, then his movements would draw Lee's attention to the northern part of the field. If Hooker could make significant gains, then all the better, for perhaps his corps could push whatever Confederate forces were there back toward the Potomac.

While Hooker moved across the creek, McClellan placed the Union IX Corps on the eastern side of the Antietam near the Lower Bridge. Thus far in the campaign, the I Corps and IX Corps had been paired together, placed in a wing command under Maj. Gen. Ambrose Burnside. Now, with Hooker's I Corps on the right, Burnside's wing structure was no more, and he and the IX Corps were positioned on the Union left.

Burnside's target was the Confederate right flank, and his attack would begin after Hooker became engaged, staggering the blows to Lee's lines on both ends of the field. Once Lee's strength

Brig. Gen. Henry Hunt served as chief of artillery for the Army of the Potomac. (loc)

Maj. Gen. Joseph Hooker, commander of the Federal I Corps, would later become the commander of the Army of the Potomac, leading it to defeat at Chancellorsville in May 1863. (loc)

While George Custer would go on to great fame as a general in the Civil War and in campaigns against Native Americans after the war, he was a young captain on George McClellan's staff at Antietam. This image shows Custer as a major general in 1865. (loc)

and positions were clear, McClellan would send the IX Corps across the creek, hopefully hitting a weakened right flank.

While the I and IX Corps were each new to McClellan, having never served under his command before, McClellan also had Maj. Gen. Edwin Sumner's II Corps and part of Maj. Gen. Fitz-John Porter's V Corps. These commands were the most familiar of McClellan's available troops, having served under him during the Peninsula campaign. Accordingly, he kept them in the Federal center along the Boonsboro Pike. Should the attacks by the I and IX Corps go according to plan, Sumner and Porter would be available for an attack up the Boonsboro Pike against the center of Lee's line. Once Maj. Gen. Joseph Mansfield arrived with the XII Corps, his men would wait in reserve. Only Maj. Gen. William Franklin and the VI Corps were absent from this plan. They were still in Pleasant Valley, guarding the Army of the Potomac against any rearguard action by Confederates coming north from Harpers Ferry through Maryland.

While McClellan's plan of attack had a role for each part of his army present on the 16th, he issued

his orders piecemeal to each of his commanding generals. McClellan did not write out any coherent orders for his army as a whole, maintaining flexibility because of the uncertainties regarding Lee's strength and his position. While this was beneficial, it also meant that the Union army had difficulties in coordinating attacks during the upcoming fight—one of the largest flaws in McClellan's leadership at Antietam.

Shortly after 3:00 p.m., the I Corps began crossing the creek. As his men spread out and advanced across the countryside, unsure of what lay to their front, Hooker grew increasingly concerned. His corps was the only sizable Union force on the west side of the creek. With the strength and precise positions of the Confederates still unknown, Hooker reiterated a request for help. McClellan, who had ridden over to meet with Hooker in person west of the Antietam, reassured the I Corps commander that he would have reinforcements by the time his men went into action the following morning.

When McClellan rode back over the Upper Bridge, he made his way to the farmhouse that Philip Pry and his family called home. There, McClellan spent the night, close enough to the front to observe and monitor the situation. Soon, he ordered Joseph Mansfield's XII Corps to cross the Antietam in support of Hooker. Mansfield's command crossed just before midnight on the 16th, making camp near the George Line farm along the Smoketown Road, just north of Hooker's position.

Brig. Gen. Fitzhugh Lee, nephew of Robert E. Lee, commanded a brigade of Confederate cavalry in the Maryland campaign. (loc)

Brig. Gen. George Meade commanded the Pennsylvania Reserve division of the Union I Corps. Less than a year after Antietam, Meade would find himself tasked with stopping another attempted invasion of the north by Lee. (loc)

Col. James Childs (standing), photographed in August 1862, was killed by an artillery shell on the morning of September 17 while serving as the acting commander of a brigade of Federal cavalry. (loc)

As a gentle rain began to fall across the landscape, it was all the men on either side could do but to peer off into the darkness, imagining where and when the battle would begin upon the dawn's first light.

* * *

The army that McClellan had at Antietam was not a well-oiled machine, but rather, one hastily cobbled together in time to meet the threat posed by Lee's invasion of Maryland. It had numerous flaws, perhaps the most glaring of which was a lack of experience, especially when

The Union signal corps positioned a station on Elk Ridge to look out across the valley toward Sharpsburg to report news of troop movements to McClellan. Elk Ridge sits just three miles east of the battlefield. (loc)

compared to the battle-hardened Army of Northern Virginia. Nowhere was this deficiency of experience more significant than the brigade commanders of each army. In the Army of Northern Virginia, 75 percent of the brigade commanders had led a brigade in combat before the battle; in the Army of the Potomac, fewer than 30 percent of the brigade commanders had any prior experience at that level.

The men in the ranks had similar problems, as well; roughly one out of every four Union soldiers had never before been in combat, while Lee's army

was composed almost entirely of veteran troops. More than 60 percent of Lee's Army of Northern Virginia had been engaged in three or more major battles; less than 10 percent of McClellan's army could say the same. While it is doubtful that McClellan knew the extent to which his army was lacking in experience, he was certainly aware of the challenges his newly created army would face in combat. Yet, with Lee and his army on Union soil, George McClellan had to work with the force that he had.

When fighting began on September 17, Robert E. Lee had roughly 40,000 men ready for battle. For decades, historians have suggested that McClellan had at least two-to-one odds over Lee at Antietam, and that the battle could have been an easy Union victory. To be sure, McClellan's army was larger, but not quite as large as historians have long held. McClellan did himself no favors by inaccurately noting in his official report that he had more than 87,000 men at the battle.

On the evening of the 16th, McClellan had sent two corps to the west side of the Antietam, totaling roughly 18,000 men. McClellan had another 36,000 men on the east side of the creek, including the II Corps, Brig. Gen. George Sykes's division of the V Corps, the IX Corps, and Federal cavalry. Overall, he had 54,000 men present that evening and when the battle began the next morning.

In Lee's army, all but one of the nine Confederate divisions were at Sharpsburg when the fighting began on September 17. For McClellan,

Originally built in the 1780s, Joshua Newcomer's house, and his barn across the street, are the only surviving structures of what was at one time a busy farm and mill complex along Antietam Creek (top). Today, the Newcomer House (bottom) serves as a local visitor center for the Heart of the Civil War Heritage Area, a cooperative agreement between the National Park Service and the Hagerstown-Washington County Convention and Visitors Bureau. It is one of the few original homes on the battlefield open to the public. (loc)(cm) he was still missing several divisions of infantry, as well as the entire VI Corps. While the VI Corps was almost 10 miles away in Pleasant Valley, and would hopefully be marching to join McClellan's force the next morning, there were no guarantees about their arrival so long as there was uncertainty over the whereabouts of Jackson's Harpers Ferry force. The only guaranteed reinforcements were those of George Morrell's V Corps division, which was just a few miles away in Keedysville. Even once these reinforcements arrived, because of the heavy combat losses Union forces suffered, at no one point did McClellan have more than 60,000 men on hand during the fighting at Antietam.

Thus, McClellan would be going to battle without his entire army, a situation which Lee was very familiar with, and one many historians seem to forget when suggesting that the battle should have been an easy victory for the Federals. When the fight began, McClellan had far fewer men than perhaps even he knew.

At the Pry House

You are currently standing at the farm of Philip Pry, east of Antietam Creek. The house was finished in 1844, and at the time of the battle, it was the home for Philip, his wife Elizabeth, and their six children. The family also had one slave, a 19-year-old girl named Georgiana. The house became a focal point for McClellan and his staff during the battle.

This is where George McClellan spent the night of September 16, 1862, on the eve of the battle. From the hillside behind the house, you can look out beyond the creek and see portions of the northern half of the battlefield.

During and after the battle, the house and its surrounding buildings were used as a hospital to

Both armies utilized the Middle Bridge over the Antietam before, during, and after the battle. This photograph is looking west from the east side of the creek, showing the rising terrain as the Boonsboro Pike runs uphill toward Sharpsburg. (loc)

treat the wounded. Union Gen. Israel Richardson was taken to a second floor bedroom after he was wounded near the Sunken Road, and was treated there until he succumbed to his wounds on November 3.

Today, the farmhouse is the site of the Pry House Field Hospital Museum, part of the National Museum of Civil War Medicine.

▶ TO STOP 2

From the Pry House, return to state route 34 (0.2 miles) and turn left. In 0.6 miles, turn left onto Keedysville Road. Note: this road crosses two narrow one-lane bridges. Proceed with caution. In 0.9 miles, you will cross the Upper Bridge over Antietam Creek. Turn left onto Mansfield Road. In 1.8 miles, turn left at the intersection onto Smoketown Road. In 0.1 miles, turn right onto Cornfield Avenue. At the stop sign in 0.4 miles, turn right onto Dunker Church Road. In 0.5 miles, follow the road as it turns to the right and becomes Mansfield Avenue. Proceed to the North Woods parking lot (on your left) in 0.2 miles. The Cornfield Trail starts from this parking lot.

Alternate Route: Note, this route follows the advance of the Union XII Corps, yet follows roads which are at times unpaved.

Upon crossing the Upper Bridge, turn right onto Keedysville Road. After going 1.7 miles, turn left onto Smoketown Road. Note, 0.4 miles in, the road narrows and becomes gravel. Be aware of potholes! After 1.6 miles turn right onto Mansfield Avenue and proceed 0.6 miles to the North Woods parking lot, which will be on your right.

GPS: N 39.48887 W 77.74719

Ready to Wake with the Dawn

CHAPTER FOUR

SEPTEMBER 16, 1862—

LATE AFTERNOON TO MIDNIGHT

As late as the afternoon of September 16, Robert E. Lee was still unsure of his next move. Encouraged by Jackson's success at Harpers Ferry, Lee now had to decide what he would do with his army once it was reunited. As fate would have it, Lee would soon have the battle he had been expecting—though not exactly as he had hoped.

Lee began that day by investigating options for moving his campaign deeper into Maryland. That morning, he sent cavalry to the north to explore this possibility while ordering his wagons to Shepherdstown, just a few miles from Sharpsburg on the other side of the Potomac in Virginia. If Jackson's men could quickly rejoin the main body of the army at Sharpsburg, Lee could either fight the Union army there, or continue toward Hagerstown to the north.

While Lee pondered that morning, the sun started to rise in the September sky, peering through the fog. Suddenly, Federal guns announced their presence on the other side of the creek. Two Union batteries were zeroing in on the Confederate center, visible on high ground around Sharpsburg. By late morning, Southern guns responded in kind.

BATTLE OF ANTIETAM—Though traditionally described as a three-phase battle, Antietam is more properly seen as a fight that took place in two phases. The northern phase of the battle began with Union attacks on the Confederate left, launched by the Federal I Corps, XII Corps, and II Corps. This phase lasted for seven hours and saw the vast majority of Antietam's casualties. The southern phase of the battle consisted of the Union left, held by the IX Corps, fighting its way across Antietam Creek and striking the Confederate right flank.

As each side traded artillery fire, Lee knew that his army was not yet ready to fight a major engagement at Sharpsburg. His army was still not full strength, numbering fewer than 30,000 men strong. Brigadier General David R. Jones's

This War Department sign shows the position of Confederate artillery at the start of the battle. (cb)

division was on the right, stretching south from the Boonsboro Turnpike; D. H. Hill's men were located north of the road to Jones's immediate left; and Brig. Gen. John Bell Hood's division was to the left of Hill, covering the left flank of the army. Brigadier General Nathan Evans's independent brigade was located on Cemetery Hill, along the Boonsboro Turnpike itself, and Maj. Gen. Jeb Stuart's cavalry division was divided, covering both of Lee's flanks.

Lee had 28 batteries of artillery spread out across his line—17 on his left and 11 on the right and center. Shortly after 8:00 a.m., Jackson arrived in Sharpsburg, and the divisions of Brig. Gen. J. R. Jones, Brig. Gen. Alexander Lawton, and Brig. Gen. John Walker were not far behind. While this was a boost to Lee, he was still awaiting the divisions of Lafayette McLaws and Maj. Gen. Richard H. Anderson. Their arrival would give Lee eight divisions of infantry, leaving only Maj. Gen. A. P. Hill's command remaining in Harpers Ferry to deal with the massive Union force which had just surrendered.

By noon, the artillery fire grew quiet and a veneer of calm fell over the battlefield. While the soldiers of the Army of Northern Virginia knew that a battle would soon be at hand, their commander was not yet certain of where or when it would occur. Lee was trying to keep his options open, yet his plans were contingent on the arrival of his Harpers Ferry divisions and word from the cavalry reconnaissance he had ordered. While he considered his options, the Union army was moving into place.

Shortly before 4:00 p.m., Lee received word that Union troops were crossing Antietam Creek in

Brig. Gen. Alpheus Williams had served as the acting commander of the XII Corps for most of the campaign leading up to Antietam. When Mansfield was mortally wounded on the morning of September 17, Williams assumed command of the corps once again. (loc)

Maj. Gen. Joseph Mansfield, XII Corps commander, graduated from West Point in 1822—seven years before Robert E. Lee. (loc)

Brig. Gen. Truman Seymour's men were involved in a skirmish in the East Woods on the night of September 16. (loc)

force at the Upper Bridge. This movement all but prevented Lee from shifting his army farther north in Maryland along the Potomac River, virtually ensuring that he would have to stand and fight at Sharpsburg or re-cross the river at Shepherdstown. Making matters worse, Federal artillery soon resumed their fire, pecking away at the Confederate position. To the south, skirmishers in D. R. Jones's division noted enemy movement near the Lower Bridge over the Antietam.

Robert E. Lee was many things as a commander, but timid was not one of them. Many generals would have seen these developments and decided that discretion was the better part of valor, not wanting to risk further losses in an already costly campaign. If McClellan's army did significant damage to Lee in Maryland, there were no guarantees the Confederates would be able to successfully slip back into Virginia. With the Potomac River just a few miles to his west, Lee would be fighting a major battle with a river to his back while facing a numerically superior enemy force.

For Robert E. Lee, deciding to stand and fight on September 16 was a gamble, but it was one he could not afford to pass up. The potential risks of battle were far more preferable than the certain costs of abandoning the campaign altogether. Lee knew that retreating in the face of the enemy would not sit well with his army. Having come so far in the campaign already, Lee still wanted to pursue the goals that had compelled him to enter Maryland two weeks earlier. If he could defeat McClellan on Union soil, it would be a stunning achievement for the South. Indeed, Lee knew that opportunity was always coupled with risk, and opportunities such as this did not come along often.

The Miller farm sits on the eastern side of the old Hagerstown Pike. David and Margaret Miller fled the farm with their children before the battle. Their house survived the fight, but their infamous cornfield was the scene of great destruction. The Park Service took possession of the property in 1990. (cm)

With Federals now on the western side of the Antietam, Lee began to move his pieces into place. Clearly, the crossing at the Upper Bridge was significant, necessitating reinforcements on the Confederate left. Having kept Jackson's men in reserve throughout the day, Lee now sent the divisions of J. R. Jones and Alexander Lawton north of Sharpsburg to his left flank, reinforcing John Bell Hood's men and leaving only the division of John Walker in reserve. At roughly the same time, Lafayette McLaws was starting his and Richard H. Anderson's divisions north from Harpers Ferry, having received

orders from Lee to hasten his arrival in Sharpsburg. Lee needed them to arrive soon, for the battle was now imminent.

Visible from the Mansfield Avenue pull-off by the North Woods, the Joseph and Mary Ann Poffenberger farm saw the Federal I Corps take position there on the night of September 16. The Park Service acquired the 120-acre property in 2000. (cm)

As Hooker's I Corps advanced west of Antietam Creek, most of the command made its way toward the Joseph Poffenberger farm, while the men of Brig. Gen. Truman Seymour's brigade were the first to encounter Confederate troops in the East Woods. Shortly before 6:00 p.m., a fight broke out between the famed Bucktails of the 13th Pennsylvania Reserve Infantry and the 9th Virginia Cavalry. As it escalated, John Bell Hood deployed his nearby infantry division, and Seymour ordered in the rest of his brigade.

Col. Stephen D. Lee commanded Confederate artillery near the Dunker Church at the start of the battle. (loc)

Maj. Gen. Jeb Stuart commanded the Army of Northern Virginia's cavalry division at Antietam. (loc)

As Seymour's men pushed southward and emerged out of the East Woods, they were subjected to artillery fire from several guns near the Dunker Church, as well as steady infantry fire from the men of Hood's command. The Pennsylvanians took shelter at the edge of the East Woods as the fight continued. There, Col. Hugh McNeil, commanding the 13th Pennsylvania Reserves, was shot through the heart, becoming the first officer to die upon the field at Antietam.

While this skirmish was intense, it did not last long. Darkness was quickly falling across the field. Seymour's brigade remained in the East Woods that night, having to wait through long hours of nervous picket duty, and to prepare for what was to come at daybreak. After the clash that evening, there was no uncertainty on either side as to what would happen the following morning. As Joe Hooker settled in for the evening at the Poffenberger farm, he was heard to tell his staff, "We are through for tonight, but tomorrow we fight the battle that will decide the fate of the Republic."

* * *

Among the things that historians today will never know is what exactly was going through the hearts and minds of the soldiers upon the field

Dedicated in 1962, the Clara Barton monument honors the efforts of "the Angel of the Battlefield" at Antietam. The monument features a cross of red brick at the base, which is made from bricks from Clara Barton's childhood home, honoring her contributions as the founder of the American Red Cross. (cm)

Clara Barton was one of the war's most famous humanitarians. Employed in the Patent Office when the war began, Barton worked to provide aid to soldiers at many battles of the war, including Antietam, where she was in field hospitals near the front lines. After the war, Barton worked to identify missing soldiers and went on to found the American Red Cross. (loc)

of Antietam on the night of September 16. After dark, a soft rain fell across the landscape, soaking the men on the front line. For many, campfires were not allowed, as the light from the flames would give away their position to the nearby enemy picket line. Brigadier General Alpheus Williams, a division commander in the XII Corps, later reflected on the tensions of that night, as he and his men made a temporary camp in the damp darkness.

I shall not, however, soon forget that night; so dark, so obscure, so mysterious, so uncertain; with the occasional rapid volleys of pickets and outposts, the low solemn sound of the command as troops came into position . . . there was a half-dreamy sensation about it all; but with a certain impression that the morrow was to be great with the future fate of our country. So much responsibility, so much intense, future anxiety! And yet I slept as soundly as though nothing was before me.

The North Woods at Antietam
(cb)

Among those waiting out the night was Maj. Rufus Dawes of the 6th Wisconsin, the great-grandson of William Dawes, who rode with Paul Revere to warn the colonists of Concord and Lexington of the British advance in April 1775. Dawes was a highly respected officer, and went on to lead the 6th Wisconsin in some of the fiercest combat of the Civil War. He later wrote of that evening: "There was a drizzling rain and with the certain prospect of deadly conflict on the morrow, the night was dismal. Nothing can be more solemn than a period of silent waiting for the summons to battle, known to be impending."

In the Confederate ranks, soldiers were reflecting on what was to come as well. Captain Francis Parker—whose artillery battery was positioned just across the Hagerstown Pike from the Dunker Church—could not help but think of the terrible nature of war itself: "As we lay down upon the field, and look up into the great sky, we can but blush for the wickedness of man . . . no man who lay upon that field and realized the deep tragedy which was to be enacted on the morrow, could not help but be sad and thoughtful. . . ."

Having engaged with Federals in the East Woods that evening, the men of John Bell Hood's division were on their last legs of exhaustion that night. Once reinforcements were deployed on Lee's left flank, Hood arranged for his men to retire to the rear for rest and food. Lieutenant James Lemon of the 18th Georgia later recalled, "We were literally famished having marched hard, fought battles and marched again on nothing but green corn in the last 3 days. We formed in the rear and waited, but the promised wagons and rations had not arrived. Thus, we lay on our arms suffering from the most severe hunger, with no recompense."

The men of Lemon's regiment were among thousands that night who lay down on the cold farmland around Sharpsburg, trying to sleep through hunger and fear. Sergeant W. H. Andrews of the 1st Georgia shared those same feelings: "At night we stretch ourselves on the ground to try and sleep off the pangs of hunger. No one knows what a day may bring forth, but from the appearance of everything tonight, thousands of poor soldiers will have no use for rations by tomorrow night."

For the soldiers on both sides, the night of September 16 was an uneasy calm before the storm. The outcome of the coming fight mattered not only to those men gathered around Sharpsburg, but to thousands of fathers, mothers, wives, brothers, sisters, and many more as well. To the young fiancé in Mississippi wondering when the next letter from her future husband would arrive; to the worried mother of two in Pennsylvania, questioning whether her children would ever see their father again. The fight the next day was to have grave consequences.

For President Lincoln in Washington, the outcome of the approaching battle would have enormous consequences as well. Nearly two months earlier, in July, Lincoln told his cabinet of his intention to issue an Emancipation Proclamation, one which would free all slaves in the Confederate states in rebellion. Having decided to wait for a Union victory before issuing such an important document, Lincoln's unsigned and unissued proclamation was dependent upon the outcome of Lee's campaign in Maryland. As he later told artist Francis Carpenter, when Lee and his army crossed into Maryland, Lincoln resolved that should the Confederates be pushed out of Union territory, he would issue his

Brig. Gen. Alexander Lawton assumed command of Richard Ewell's division following the latter's wounding at Second Manassas. Lawton's division was positioned just south of the Cornfield when the battle began on the morning of September 17. (loc)

Emancipation Proclamation. For Lincoln—and for millions of people held as slaves—the impending battle was to forever change the course of history.

As thousands of soldiers rested in the fields around Sharpsburg, Lincoln spent the night in Washington, waiting for word from the front. As always, in the morning it was to be common men who would decide not just the fate of the battle but the fate of freedom itself. Prior to the war, these men had been farmers, doctors, shoemakers, husbands, fathers, and brothers. Now, they were to be soldiers in the bloodiest day in American history, deciding the future fate of millions born and unborn. And that night they slept in the fields around a small farming town in western Maryland. As historian Bruce Catton wrote, "And whatever it may be that nerves men to die for a flag or a phrase or a man or an inexpressible dream was drowsing with them, ready to wake with the dawn."

At the North Woods

The North Woods is where much of the I Corps was located on the night of September 16. The visitor center is approximately one mile to the south. From this position, visitors can gain a key understanding of the terrain on the northern half of Antietam National Battlefield, understanding why the opening hours of the battle were so costly.

The parking area is located just south of the Joseph Poffenberger farm, the home of Joseph and Mary Ann Poffenberger. The couple had no children of their own, and when the armies approached Sharpsburg, they fled before the battle. Unfortunately, like so many others, the Poffenberger's farm suffered significantly during the fight. They lost all their food stores, many of their fences were burned, and most of their belongings were taken. Joseph filed damage claims for his losses, but never received compensation.

To Stop 3

From the North Woods parking lot, head east (toward the row of soldier monuments) on Mansfield Avenue for 0.5 miles. At the stop sign, turn right onto Smoketown Road. Continue 0.2 miles and turn right onto Cornfield Avenue (East Woods parking lot will be on your right). Proceed 0.3 miles to the Cornfield tour stop, where the parking lot will be to the right.

GPS: N 39.48091 W 77.74734

The Cornfield

CHAPTER FIVE

SEPTEMBER 17, 1862—DAWN TO 9 A.M.

In the predawn hours of September 17, the armies awoke from their uneasy slumber. The sounds of camp and preparations for battle mixed together, as canteens and cartridges were each prepared for the day ahead. In the 128th Pennsylvania—a new regiment which had never before seen combat—Pvt. Frederick Crouse recalled the stillness in the ranks that morning as "the calm that proceeds a terrible storm." With no time or inclination for breakfast, Private Crouse opened his Bible and read the 91st Psalm. He no doubt took comfort from the seventh verse: "A thousand may fall at your side, ten thousand at your right hand, but it will not come near you." Though Private Crouse would be severely wounded in the shoulder that morning, unlike thousands of others, he lived to see his family again.

In the early mist of dawn, the picket fire of the two armies began to slowly crescendo, rising with the sun itself. Artillery fire soon began to punctuate the roll of musketry. Captain Albert Monroe of the 1st Rhode Island Light Artillery, positioned near the farm of Joseph Poffenberger, remembered the scene with vivid imagery:

Capt. James Stewart's Battery B, 4th U.S. Artillery, sat just west of the Hagerstown Pike. (cb)

It was the early gray light that appeared just before the sun rises above the horizon, and we could little more than distinguish each other. We had not half finished

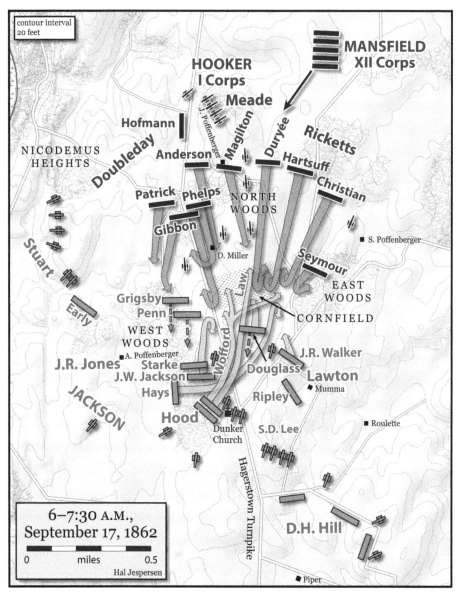

MANSFIELD
XII Corps

HOOKER
I Corps

Meade

Hofmann

J. Poffenberger

Magilton

Duryée

Ricketts

NICODEMUS
HEIGHTS

Doubleday

Anderson

Poffenberger

Hartsuff

Christian

Patrick   Phelps   NORTH
WOODS

Gibbon

S. Poffenberger

D. Miller

Seymour

Lawton

EAST
WOODS

CORNFIELD

Stuart

Grigsby

Penn

Early

WEST
WOODS

A. Poffenberger

Wofford

J.R. Walker

Douglass   Lawton

J.R. Jones   Starke
J.W. Jackson

Mumma

JACKSON

Hays

Ripley

Hood

Roulette

Dunker
Church

S.D. Lee

6–7:30 A.M.,
September 17, 1862

Hagerstown Turnpike

D.H. Hill

0   miles   0.5

Hal Jespersen

Piper

6 A.M. SEPTEMBER 17, 1862—Miller's Cornfield saw the bloodiest fighting of Antietam, beginning at dawn on the 17th. Major General Joseph Hooker deployed two divisions from his I Corps, which advanced south and engaged with several Confederate divisions in a fierce back and forth battle.

our meal . . . and we could see the first rays of the sun lighting up the distant hilltops, when there was a sudden flash, and the air around us appeared to be alive with shot and shell from the enemy's artillery. The opposing hill seemed suddenly to have become an active volcano, belching forth flame and smoke.

With those shells, Monroe witnessed the opening salvos of the bloodiest day in American history, a constant array of thunder and carnage that would last for the next 12 hours.

*   *   *

Joe Hooker was up before dawn on the morning of September 17, determined to open the battle with a strong assault. As he rode up to the Union picket line, he peered south across the rolling farmland, spotting several notable landmarks. Among them was the Dunker Church, which sat alongside the Hagerstown Pike as it ran southward towards the town of Sharpsburg. Across the road from the church, there was a large and notable plateau covered by several batteries of Confederate artillery. As the gunners of each side prepared for the task ahead, Hooker realized that whichever army held the plateau across from the Dunker Church would control the northern half of the battlefield. Hooker determined to push his corps southward to wrest the high ground from the Confederates. He would attack southward within the hour.

Maj. Gen. James Ricketts, a veteran officer whose I Corps division opened the fighting in the eastern half of the Cornfield, had been captured and wounded at First Manassas. He was held as a prisoner of war for seven months before he was returned in a prisoner exchange. (loc)

The ground south of Hooker's position was largely open and surrounded by three wooded areas. The I Corps was encamped just north of the North Woods, the smallest of these woodlots. South of the North Woods, the terrain opened into pastured fields, running several hundred yards to a large cornfield owned by David Miller. While this cornfield was not unique prior to the battle, it has been henceforth known as "The Cornfield" because of the slaughter that occurred there; it will be referred to accordingly here. The eastern edge of the Cornfield was bordered by the East Woods, where the skirmish fighting on the night of September 16 had taken place. On its western boundary, the Cornfield extended to the Hagerstown Pike. Across the road to the west lay the West Woods, which extended southward toward the Dunker Church.

The ground south of the Cornfield was open, running all the way to the plateau opposite the

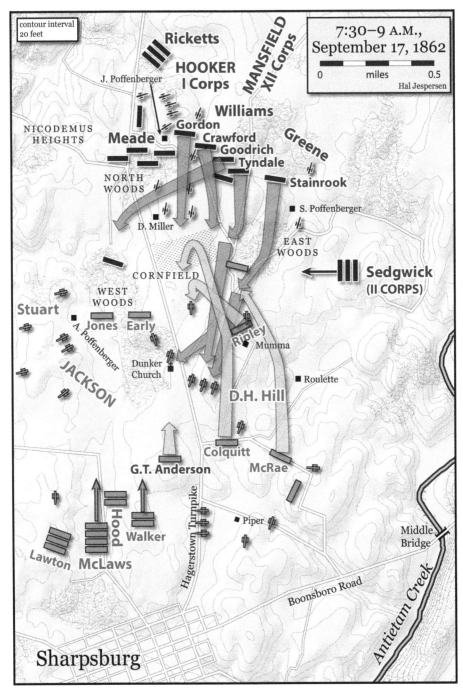

6 A.M. SEPTEMBER 17, 1862—By 7:30 a.m., the Federal XII Corps had deployed into Miller's Cornfield and the East Woods, engaging remnants of Gen. John Bell Hood's division, as well as several brigades from the command of Gen. D. H. Hill which had been sent north to reinforce Lee's left flank.

Dunker Church where Confederate gunners had established a strong position. The Cornfield itself was on elevated terrain and easily visible to artillerymen from both sides. Essentially, any southward push meant that Hooker would be sending his men through open and elevated ground bordered by three woodlots and subjected to a brutal crossfire from Confederate artillery that was positioned on nearby Nicodemus Heights, protecting the far left flank of the Confederates. There are many reasons why the first hours of Antietam were the bloodiest, and the terrain around the Cornfield is foremost among them.

Brig. Gen. Abner Doubleday was one of the defenders of Fort Sumter and allegedly fired the first shot back at the Confederates on April 12, 1861. Doubleday is also rumored to have invented baseball, though that has been proven untrue. Doubleday's I Corps division was fighting along the Hagerstown Pike early on the morning of September 17. (loc)

Making matters worse for Hooker's men, they would be advancing against some of the best soldiers in Lee's army. Fresh off their success at Harpers Ferry, Lee's left flank was held by the men of Stonewall Jackson's command, with the famed Jackson himself overseeing their fight. On the west side of the Hagerstown Pike in the West Woods, Jackson had four brigades of infantry positioned, representing the entire division of J. R. Jones. The first line, consisting of two brigades, was under the command of Col. A. J. Grigsby of the 27th Virginia. Just over 200 yards behind them were two more Confederate brigades, these led by Brig. Gen. William Starke. While these were experienced troops, they were weary from the strain of battle in the weeks preceding Antietam; Jones's division numbered under 3,000 men.

On the eastern side of the road, just south of Miller's Cornfield, were several more brigades of Confederate infantry in the division of Alexander Lawton, which had been previously led by Richard Ewell, who was wounded at Second Manassas. On the left of the line was Lawton's former brigade, now led by Col. Marcellus Douglass. To his right was Col. James Walker's brigade, previously commanded by Isaac Trimble, who was also absent due to wounds. Behind the front line, near the Dunker Church, were Brig. Gen. Harry Hays's men, known as the "Louisiana Tigers."

Altogether, Jackson had more than 7,000 men south of the Cornfield and around the East Woods

"The piles of dead on the Sharpsburg and Hagerstown Turnpike were frightful. The 'angle of death' at Spotsylvania, and the Cold Harbor 'slaughter pen,' and the Fredericksburg Stone Wall, where Sumner charged, were all mentally compared by me, when I saw them, with this turnpike at Antietam. My feeling was that the Antietam Turnpike surpassed all in manifest evidence of slaughter."
— Maj. Rufus Dawes, 6th Wisconsin (loc)

and West Woods. Add in the exposed terrain and the Confederates' advantage in artillery positions and Lee's left flank was well defended that morning.

Hooker intended to counter this defense with a two-pronged assault. With the high ground opposite of the Dunker Church as his objective, Hooker ordered the division of Maj. Gen. Abner Doubleday to advance south along the Hagerstown Pike, heading directly toward his target. Doubleday had four brigades, making his the largest division in the I Corps.

To Doubleday's left, Hooker ordered Maj. Gen. James Ricketts's division into the Cornfield and the East Woods to the support of Seymour's men, who were sparring with Walker's brigade from their advanced position in the East Woods. Though Ricketts's division was not far to Doubleday's left, the ground sloped downward in the eastern half of the Cornfield, meaning that the two divisions would be operating largely independent of one another.

Capt. John Pelham commanded Maj. Gen. Jeb Stuart's horse artillery and played a key role in the Confederate defense of Nicodemus Heights early in the battle. (loc)

Brig. Gen. John Bell Hood, a native Kentuckian, led a division of battle-hardened veterans at Antietam. (loc)

Pvt. Julius Rabardy of the 12th Massachusetts was severely wounded in the leg in the Cornfield. He found himself caught between the opposing lines of fire. Rabardy, who survived the battle and the war, later wrote that at Antietam, he was "exposed to the fire of slavery and freedom." (Photo courtesy of the Manchester Historical Museum).

Shortly before 6:00 a.m., Ricketts's men were moving southward, and Confederate artillery opened on their advance as soon as it was visible. The incoming fire rattled the nerves of the men, most of whom steadied themselves and continued on. Colonel William Christian was not among them. Commanding one of Ricketts's brigades, Christian snapped that morning. When his men came under fire, Christian began ordering several parade ground marching maneuvers, after which he fled toward the rear and out of the fight. Nearby, another of Ricketts's brigade commanders, Brig. Gen. George Hartsuff, was struck by a shell fragment.

Before his attack was even underway, Ricketts had lost two of his three brigade commanders, delaying those brigades and leaving only the command of Brig. Gen. Abram Duryee pushing south into the Cornfield at 6:00 a.m. With Federal infantry pushing southward, several artillery batteries positioned themselves north of the Cornfield to support their advance.

Duryee's brigade was composed of New Yorkers and Pennsylvanians, and was just over 1,000 men strong that morning. As the Federals marched through the head-high corn, they were unsure of

The Texas Monument was dedicated on November 11, 1964. Brig. Gen. William Wofford's Texas Brigade took heavy losses fighting here on the morning of September 17. (cb)

where the Confederate battle line was posted. All doubt was erased when they reached the southern fence of the Cornfield and were greeted with a blistering round of musket fire from Col. Marcellus Douglass's Georgians just 200 yards to their front. "The lines melted away like wax," recalled one of the Federals. Douglass's men suffered heavily as well, taking artillery fire from guns positioned just north of the Cornfield. Douglass himself was killed during the fight.

With Duryee's men taking heavy fire, Hartsuff's brigade, now led by Col. Richard Coulter of the 11th Pennsylvania, pushed southward to take up the fight. Stretching from the Cornfield into the East Woods, Coulter's line was hit by what remained of Douglass's Georgians and Colonel Walker's brigade, both of which were sustaining heavy losses from the hammer-like blows of the I Corps infantry and artillery. Fortunately for the Confederates, Harry Hays's brigade was on its way.

An eclectic mix of ethnicities and backgrounds, Hays's men were among the best fighters in Lee's army. Their advance placed them on a collision course with Coulter's men, joining together with the remnants of Douglass's command to drive into the Federals. In the course of the action, both lines suffered heavily. Private George Kimball of the 12th Massachusetts wrote that the withering fire turned the Confederate battle line into "squads and stumps." With Coulter's own ranks thinning by the minute as well, Christian's brigade finally arrived at the front, now led by Col. Peter Lyle of the 90th Pennsylvania.

While Ricketts's men smashed into the right and center of Lawton's division, Doubleday's men pressed south along the Hagerstown Pike, with Brig. Gen. John Gibbon's brigade leading the way. Gibbon's command consisted of regiments from Wisconsin and Indiana, and their excellent combat record had earned them the nickname "Iron Brigade." As Gibbon's men pushed south, with Battery B, 4th U.S. Artillery in support, they were hit by Confederate fire from both the east and west sides of the Hagerstown Pike, forcing Gibbon to split his brigade in two, sending the 7th Wisconsin and 19th Indiana to the West Woods, with the 2nd and 6th Wisconsin into the Cornfield itself.

Gibbon's advance was supported by two more brigades, those of Col. Walter Phelps and Brig. Gen. Marsena Patrick. Phelps's men veered to the east of the road while Patrick's men turned to the west. Thus, Doubleday's fight consisted of clearing Confederate forces on both sides of the Hagerstown Pike.

The Confederate front line in the West Woods— consisting of Winder's and Jones's brigades— did not hold for long thanks to canister fire from Battery B and the pressure of the Iron Brigade, leaving the second line under William Starke to swing into action. Starke's men pushed through an open clover field toward the Hagerstown Pike, delivering a blistering fire into Gibbon's left. In response, Gibbon's men swung to their right, and with support from Colonel Phelps's command, the two lines blazed away at each other from across the road at a distance of less than 50 yards. While the Confederates put up a valiant effort, they could not withstand this fire for long, especially with the rest of Gibbon's men and Patrick's brigade pushing against their now-exposed left flank. Men were gunned down along the fence line, and the slaughter was filling the road itself. During this fight, Starke's battle line was devastated, losing nearly 500 men. Ten officers were killed, including Starke himself, who was mortally wounded and became the first of six generals to die at Antietam.

At this point, the battle was just over one hour old. By 7:00 a.m., over 3,000 casualties had fallen at the rate of roughly one casualty per second of fighting. Four divisions—two Union and two Confederate—had been virtually destroyed. Hooker's initial advance had bloodied the Confederates and staggered Jackson's defensive lines, but Confederate reinforcements were on their way.

After their engagement with the Pennsylvanians of Truman Seymour's brigade the night before, John Bell Hood's division had been pulled back from the

Cpl. John Morton Booker, Company I, 23rd Virginia, was mortally wounded near the Cornfield, and later died of his wounds at the Grove Farm. (loc)

front lines to rest and finally receive their rations. This was done, however, upon the agreement that if they were needed the next morning, they would come into the fight when ordered. Now, with the sounds of battle growing around them, the men of Hood's command were finally cooking their breakfast behind the lines, hoping that they would be allowed to rest instead of fight. That would not be their fate.

One Virginia soldier described Miller's Cornfield as "those corn acres of hell." (cb)

When the orders came to move out, Lt. James Lemon of the 18th Georgia recalled the anger felt by the men as they rushed into battle once again:

To our everlasting dismay, the firing from the field from which we had withdrawn had greatly intensified and we were ordered back to the front at once. Our men went almost wild with anger and furiously threw their rations to the ground and poured out their coffee as they moved into line. General Wofford had ridden up and was among us as we formed, calling out 'Never mind boys, there will be plenty to eat soon enough. It is the Yankees who have taken your breakfast. Make them pay for it!' A savage yell went up in response and the men's faces I shall never forget. Wild-eyed and furious, clenched teeth and oaths from every man, from the most savage to the most mild-hearted, all were as one in their wrath. They were like savage Devils from the Infernal regions, howling madly and looking for a fight.

Hood's two veteran brigades, commanded by Brig. Gen. William Wofford and Col. Evander Law, swept across the body-strewn ground north of the Dunker Church, slamming into the Federal troops in the Cornfield. Wofford's men were on the left of the advance, with Law on the right.

As Law's men swung toward the East Woods, they landed a devastating blow on the remnants of Ricketts's division. From across the Smoketown Road, men of Brig. Gen. Roswell Ripley's brigade had been adding their fire to the mix, and now, with Law's arrival, they augmented the withering fire tearing apart the Federal line, forcing the Union troops to fall back into the woods.

Encouraged by the Union retreat, some of Law's soldiers pushed through the blood-covered cornstalks and reached the northern fence line of Miller's field, finding that Brig. Gen. George Meade's Pennsylvania Reserves were immediately to their front. Once the Southerners were visible,

The southern boundary of David Miller's Cornfield (cb)

sheets of musket fire poured into their ranks. The Federal line had additional artillery support, tearing into Law's men while the Confederates put up a valiant fight.

To Law's left, Wofford's men pushed through the weakened Federal lines along the Hagerstown Pike. Rufus Dawes of the 6th Wisconsin recalled that the Southern musket fire was "like a scythe running through our line." Dawes later noted that this fighting "was the most dreadful slaughter to which our regiment was subjected in the war."

Most of Wofford's brigade swung to the left and pushed toward Gibbon's and Patrick's men, as well as the guns of Battery B, all of which were on the west side of the road. Alongside the musket fire, the guns of Battery B were firing double rounds of canister into the Confederate lines with a devastating effect, slowing the Southern advance. In the Hampton Legion, several flag bearers fell in quick order. The Legion's commander, Lt. Col. M. W. Gary, saw Maj. J. H. Dingle pick up the flag and shout, "Legion, follow your colors!" as he rushed toward the enemy lines. As Gary wrote, "The words had an inspiring effect, and the men rallied bravely under their flag, fighting desperately at every step." Major Dingle was struck down moments later.

While most of Wofford's command was

attacking the Federals along the Hagerstown Pike, the 1st Texas pressed straight ahead through the Cornfield itself. Waving its battle flag proudly, the 1st Texas rushed into the corn, unaware that along the northern fence line Lt. Col. Robert Anderson's brigade of Pennsylvanians lay in wait. When the Texans passed the mid-point of the Cornfield, Capt. Dunbar Ransom's battery opened on them, and when they closed to within 30 yards of the Pennsylvanians, Anderson's men unleashed fearful volleys into their ranks. In mere moments, the Texans were devastated. Eight different color bearers were gunned down, and the regiment lost 182 of its 226 men. Two entire companies ceased to exist. The surviving Texans fled back across the blood-soaked ground, their beloved Lone Star flag grabbed up as a trophy by a Pennsylvania soldier.

Meade's deployment provided the necessary reinforcements to break the tide of Hood's advance in the Cornfield, although Hood's men had done their damage. After just an hour and a half of battle, Hooker's I Corps was in shambles. Regiments were torn apart, commanders were missing, and very few men remained to continue the attacks. Hooker had lost over 2,500 men in the Cornfield fighting, yet the Confederates had been punished as well. Lawton and Jones had suffered a combined 2,000 casualties, and Hood's command had been cut in half in less than an hour.

With Hood's massive losses, more Confederates were soon on their way to reinforce Lee's deteriorating left flank. The nearest division was that of D. H. Hill, which was spread out from the Mumma Farm to the Boonsboro Pike. Hill's five brigades had been engaged three days earlier at South Mountain, and all five would again be thrown into the fray at Antietam. The closest brigade was that of Roswell Ripley, whose men had been firing into and around the East Woods for some time that morning. Ripley's men had set the Mumma house ablaze earlier that day, preventing it from becoming a safe haven for Federal sharpshooters. As Hood's lines melted away under the withering Federal pressure, Ripley's

Confederate dead along the Hagerstown Pike (loc)

brigade pushed north from the Mumma farm, taking position south of the Cornfield.

As Confederate reinforcements arrived in the Cornfield, Hooker's I Corps now received help of its own. Finally, the XII Corps was being thrown into the fight, with its new corps commander Maj. Gen. Joseph Mansfield. Mansfield had a long military career and was a veteran officer, though he had not seen much action thus far in the war. In fact, he had only taken command of the XII Corps on September 15. Mansfield's corps was the smallest in McClellan's army, and it suffered from severe problems of inexperience. Of the five brigade commanders in the XII Corps at Antietam, four of them took command of their brigade in September 1862. Many of these brigades had green regiments that were large in size and lacking any experience at all. Some of the men and officers were unfamiliar with basic marching commands.

As the XII Corps deployed that morning, Mansfield was at the front, placing regiments into line of battle himself. Having positioned the 10th Maine and gone to bring up another regiment, Mansfield was caught off guard when the Maine men began firing in the direction of what he believed were Union soldiers. No sooner had Mansfield realized that his men were firing at

A mortuary cannon marks where Brig. Gen. William Starke was killed near the Hagerstown Pike during the first hour of fighting at Antietam. (cb)

Brig. Gen. Samuel W. Crawford was an army surgeon on duty at Fort Sumter when the war began. Though he was a brigade commander at Antietam, he took temporary command of his division when Alpheus Williams assumed command of the XII Corps upon Mansfield's mortal wounding. Crawford was wounded shortly afterwards, though he survived and went on to lead a division of Pennsylvania Reserves at Gettysburg the following year. (loc)

Capt. Robert Gould Shaw, 2nd Massachusetts, saw combat in the Cornfield later in the morning on September 17. After Antietam, he became the commander of the 54th Massachusetts, the first African American raised in the North to serve in the Union army during the Civil War. (loc)

Brig. Gen. Alfred Colquitt was a congressman from Georgia before the Civil War and a delegate at Georgia's secession convention in 1861. His brigade lost 722 men in the Cornfield at Antietam—more than 50 percent of his command. After the war, Colquitt served as the governor of Georgia and a U.S. senator from Georgia. (loc)

Confederates than he was shot in the chest by an enemy bullet. Mansfield was brought back from the front and carried by ambulance to the George Line farmhouse to the north along the Smoketown Road. He died there the following day, becoming the highest-ranking officer to die at Antietam.

Mansfield's wounding led to a command shakeup in the XII Corps. Brigadier General Alpheus Williams, who had commanded the corps for most of the campaign, was its leader once again. As he deployed the men into battle, Confederates in Roswell Ripley's brigade pushed directly into the Cornfield. There, they encountered the men of Brig. Gen. George Gordon's XII Corps brigade. While the two sides staggered each other, additional Federal support came along the Hagerstown Pike, pressing into Ripley's flank and forcing him to withdraw.

As Ripley's men fell back, Brig. Gen. Alfred Colquitt and Duncan McRae arrived, the last of the reserves from D. H. Hill's division. Colonel Duncan McRae was not the brigade's normal commander;

The monument to slain XII Corps commander Joseph Mansfield sits not along Mansfield Avenue, but rather at the intersection of Smoketown Road and Mansfield Monument Road. The monument was erected by the state of Connecticut and dedicated on May 24, 1900. (cm)

A mortuary cannon marks the area where Maj. Gen. Joseph Mansfield was mortally wounded in the East Woods. (cb)

he only assumed his position as a result of Brig. Gen. Samuel Garland's death on South Mountain three days before. There, Garland's men had been in a fearsome crossfire, sustaining heavy losses.

Now under McRae, the brigade was positioned near the East Woods when a large Federal presence was spotted on its flank, causing great panic and fears of a repeat of South Mountain. McRae's men fled the field, leaving only the remnants of Hood's division and Alfred Colquitt's brigade to hold the Cornfield. These remaining Confederates were taking fire from Federal artillery, yet they still held their ground. They could not hold for long, though, because yet another Federal division was soon bearing down on the East Woods.

At age 61, Brig. Gen. George Sears Greene was among the older generals on the field. His division was just over 2,500 men strong, consisting of three brigades, one of which—commanded by Col. William Goodrich—was detached from his command and sent to the Hagerstown Pike to reinforce parts of the I Corps. With his remaining two brigades—commanded by Col. Henry Stainrook and Lt. Col. Hector Tyndale—Greene advanced through the

East Woods and emerged directly on the flank of the Confederate line. Tyndale's brigade swung into Colquitt's men, striking the 6th Georgia directly on the flank. Captain John Hanna of the 6th Georgia noted the incoming fire on the regiment's flank, and no sooner had he alerted Lt. Col. James Newton of the threat than both officers were struck dead by

The artillery battery of 24-year-old Capt. Joseph Knap, part of the Federal XII Corps, was engaged near the Smoketown Road on the morning of September 17, 1862. (loc)

musket fire from the 66th Ohio. While Tyndale pressured Colquitt, Col. Henry Stainrook swung farther to the south, pushing his brigade along the Smoketown Road.

With Greene's strong advance, Colquitt's men fell back, along with some parts of Ripley's command which had stayed in the fight. At this time, all three brigades that D. H. Hill had sent north had been repulsed. Greene's men continued advancing southward along the Smoketown Road and took up position just to the south of it in a swale of ground on the Mumma farmstead.

By this point, the Federal advance had pushed Confederate forces deep into the West Woods, and Confederate artillery had fallen back from Nicodemus Heights to Hauser Ridge and Reel Ridge, where they were no longer under the threat of the I Corps artillery.

This was the largest and most significant breakthrough of the battle thus far, and indeed, one of the best that would occur that day. As Hooker rode forward toward the Smoketown Road, he was hopeful that the remnants of his and Mansfield's commands could smash the remaining Confederate resistance on the northern end of the field. Hooker would not be a part of any further fighting, however, as he was struck in the foot by a bullet, and had to be removed from the field due to loss of blood. His day was done, and George Meade became the acting commander of the I Corps.

At this point, it is important to pause and take note of what had occurred thus far in the battle. Two Federal corps and parts of four Confederate divisions had been thrown into and around the

Cornfield, nearly all of which were virtually destroyed after heavy casualties sustained in the fighting. In the span of just over three hours, David Miller's Cornfield had been transformed into a scene of unimaginable slaughter.

Writing in his official report on the battle, Joseph Hooker provided some of the most memorable and oft-quoted lines describing the sight of the Cornfield: "In the time I am writing, every stalk of corn in the northern and greater part of the field was cut as closely as could have been done with a knife, and the slain lay in rows precisely as they stood in their ranks a few moments before. It was never my fortune to witness a more bloody, dismal battlefield."

Confederate guns face north toward the Cornfield. (cb)

Hooker's description was echoed by countless others, including Edward Bragg of the 6th Wisconsin. Bragg recalled the scenes near the Hagerstown Pike as being "too terrible to behold without a shock. . . . I counted eighty Rebels in one row along the fence in front of us, lying so thick you could step from one to the other, and this was only in one place. In others they lay in heaps, mowed down, and many of our brave boys with them. So it was everywhere."

For the Confederates, the scene was just as ghastly. Each division engaged had seen its ranks torn apart by shot and shell. D. H. Hill's three brigades lost more than 1,500 casualties, while Hood's losses came to more than 1,000 men—50 percent of his division. In the fight to defend its left flank, the Army of Northern Virginia had lost nearly 4,000 soldiers by 9:00 a.m. Similarly, the I Corps and XII Corps had a combined loss of more than 4,000 men during that same time span. In just over three hours of combat, there had been roughly 8,000 combined casualties around the Cornfield.

The comparisons to other Civil War battles are shocking. The Cornfield fighting alone either eclipsed or approximated the total battle casualties of both armies from First Manassas, South

One of the most distinctive monuments on the battlefield honors the 90th Pennsylvania. Three stacked rifles, with bayonets affixed, hold a pot over a campfire. The monument, which sits along Cornfield Avenue, describes the location as "a hot place." (cm)

Mountain, Malvern Hill, Perryville, Glendale, Kennesaw Mountain, Peachtree Creek, and the battle of the Crater at Petersburg. On its own, the fighting in the Cornfield stands as one of the most costly fights of the Civil War. Yet, the Cornfield was not its own battle. It was only the opening chapter of the bloodiest day in American history.

At the Cornfield

From the parking lot at park Auto Stop 4, the Cornfield Trail can be seen running through the middle of the Cornfield. This 1.5-mile trail highlights the Union advance and is accessible from both the Cornfield Stop and the North Woods. The monuments along Cornfield Avenue highlight units from the I, XII, and VI Corps, all of which held this part of the field at some point on the day of the battle. Recent preservation efforts have led to the acquisition of the ground just south of Cornfield Avenue, where Lawton's men were positioned when the fight opened that morning. At the time of publication, this ground is still owned by the Civil War Trust.

Looking north of the Cornfield, you will find the ground rising to a ridgeline. It was in this vicinity in 2008 where a hiker came across a groundhog hole that had unearthed the remains of a 19-year-old soldier from New York. After the National Park Service excavated the area, the soldier's remains were transported to Saratoga National Cemetery in New York for burial.

In the days after the battle, the dead of both sides were buried where they fell on the field. While efforts were later made to move Union dead to the Antietam National Cemetery and Confederate dead to three local cemeteries, as this story from 2008 shows, not all of the soldiers were found, and many may still be out on the battlefield. Because of this, it is important to be respectful and mindful that Antietam is still the final resting place for many who gave their lives there.

▶ To Stop 4

From the Cornfield parking lot, continue west toward the Dunker Church Road and turn left (<0.1 miles). In 0.2 miles, turn right into Philadelphia Brigade Park. The parking area surrounds the monument to your front.

GPS: N 39.47843 W 77.74921

The West Woods

CHAPTER SIX

SEPTEMBER 17, 1862—9 A.M. TO 10 A.M.

Throughout the morning of September 17, Robert E. Lee was consistently facing staggering blows to his left flank, forcing him to use his reserves much sooner than he had anticipated. The first several hours of the battle saw Lee repeatedly sending more and more of his forces to the Cornfield, plugging holes as they occurred. If his flank was driven back far enough, Lee knew he may have to leave the field. He was resolved to do anything he could to prevent that from occurring.

Lee's actions on September 17 were some of the finest of his military career. Though he typically allowed his subordinates to dictate the tactical course of a battle, at Antietam Lee himself became involved in the fighting. He did so out of necessity, realizing the high stakes involved. His army faced the possibility of total destruction, but it also had the opportunity of victory on Union soil, which would have changed the course of the war.

While many claim Lee was at his finest seven months later at Chancellorsville in May 1863, his performance on the day of the battle at Antietam in September 1862 ranks among Lee's greatest moments of the war. He displayed grace under pressure as few commanders have ever done.

By the time the Confederates were driven from the Cornfield for good, Lee was already

The 125th Pennsylvania Monument honors a rookie regiment from the XII Corps. The men of the 125th Pennsylvania took the brunt of the Confederate counterattack in the West Woods. (cb)

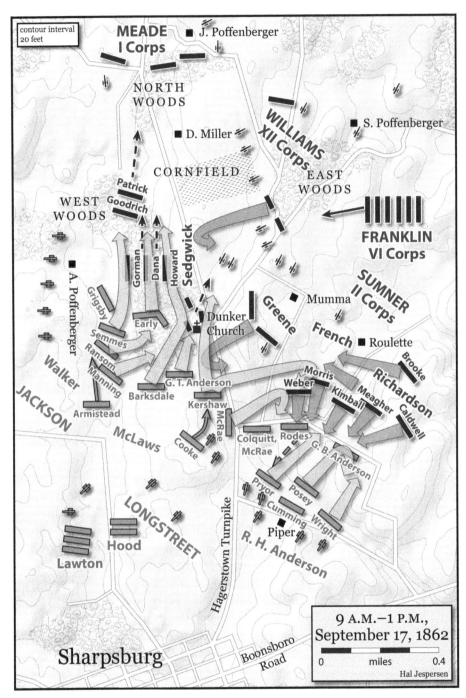

9 A.M.-1 P.M. SEPTEMBER 17, 1862—Over the span of four hours, the three divisions of Maj. Gen. Edwin Sumner's II Corps launched attacks stretching from the West Woods to the Sunken Road. The II Corps lost roughly one third of its strength, being hit by numerous Confederate counterattacks across its lines.

working on strengthening his lines once again. Just before the battle began, Lafayette McLaws and Richard Anderson had finally arrived from Harpers Ferry with their divisions. Upon arriving, McLaws himself had fallen asleep in some tall grass west of Sharpsburg because of his exhaustion from the rigorous campaign. While he slept, his men were placed in reserve getting their own much needed respite.

That rest, however, was soon broken by the necessities of the battle. With Lee looking to reinforce his left, McLaws was roused from his slumber and his division was ordered northward. In addition to McLaws, Lee drew John Walker's division from his far-right flank, where it had been guarding Snavely's Ford over the Antietam, and sent it towards his left as well. Lee also took the brigade of Brig. Gen. George T. Anderson from James Longstreet's command and sent it to Jackson in the West Woods. Altogether, Lee was sending over 7,000 men to strengthen his left just as a new threat was forming—one they were perfectly positioned to meet.

Maj. Gen. Edwin V. Sumner was the oldest general in either army at Antietam. (loc)

*   *   *

Early on the morning of the 17th, Maj. Gen. Edwin Sumner was impatiently awaiting his orders at the Pry House. At 65 years old, Sumner was the oldest general in either army at Antietam. He enlisted in the United States army in 1819, seven years before George McClellan was even born. By the time of Antietam, Sumner had a long military career behind him, and he was the commander of the II Corps, the largest in the Army of the Potomac at over 15,000 men strong. Sumner's command was divided into three divisions, two of which—those of John Sedgwick and Israel Richardson—were full of veteran troops. His third division, commanded by William French, was assembled during the Maryland campaign with mostly rookie soldiers.

Sumner's men began that day on the eastern side of the Antietam as a part of McClellan's

Maj. Gen. John Sedgwick would survive grievous wounds at Antietam only to be killed on May 9, 1864, at the battle of Spotsylvania. He would be, by that time, the highest-ranking Union officer killed in the war. (loc)

Brig. Gen. Oliver O. Howard, commander of the "Philadelphia Brigade" which consisted of the 69th, 71st, 72nd, and 106th Pennsylvania regiments, lost 545 casualties in the fighting in the West Woods. (loc)

Brig. Gen. Willis Gorman's men led the advance of Sedgwick's division into the West Woods at Antietam. (loc)

reserves. McClellan seemed to favor the II Corps because of its experience fighting under his command on the Peninsula, and thus he kept them out of the initial fighting to use in the event of a breakthrough in Lee's lines.

At 7:20 a.m., with combat raging in the Cornfield, McClellan ordered Sumner to take his command across the Antietam and reinforce the Federal effort against Lee's left, though he could only advance with two of his three divisions for the time being. Israel Richardson's command was to remain behind until George Morrell's division of the V Corps arrived near the Pry House, taking its place along the Boonsboro Pike and in general reserve. Thus, Sumner advanced with Sedgwick and French in the lead, with Richardson to follow later.

Sumner's men were on the move shortly after receiving their orders, crossing the Antietam at Pry's Ford and heading west toward the battlefield. On his approach to the field, Sumner came across Hooker, who was then being carried to the rear because of his wound. It is not clear what Hooker conveyed to Sumner regarding the state of affairs at the front. Hooker later stated that he was only partially conscious at the time from loss of blood. Shortly after meeting with Hooker, Sumner received orders from army headquarters directing him to move into the East Woods as soon as possible. He pressed on, arriving in the woods by 9:00 a.m., discovering a war-torn landscape.

As Sumner arrived, he took stock of what he could see. Clearly, the first several hours had been ferocious; the fields to his front were littered with thousands of bodies. He was soon met by George Meade, now the acting commander of the I Corps, who provided more information on the fighting thus far. To his left, Sumner noticed the two brigades of Greene's division south of the East Woods near the Mumma farm. After performing a reconnaissance of the area, Sumner determined that occupying the West Woods was key to holding the northern end of the field. That is where Confederates were last seen in force, and Sumner resolved to pursue them.

Because of Greene's location, Sumner believed he had strong support on his flank, and that the West Woods would be an easy target for his men. He ordered Sedgwick's men to push west into the West Woods, driving back whatever Confederate forces remained there. Accordingly, as French followed Sedgwick onto the field, he was ordered to move to the left of Greene's men. Sumner and his staff had noticed a Confederate presence beyond the Mumma farm, necessitating a Federal push in that direction to clear Greene's flank. While this thinking and these orders seem simple enough, Greene's presence effectively split the II Corps in two, opening two separate fights that each cost Sumner heavy casualties. Indeed, between the impending combat in the West Woods and the Sunken Road, Sumner's command would suffer higher losses than any other corps at Antietam.

Brig. Gen. Napoleon Jackson Tecumseh Dana coincidentally shared names with three other military leaders and a future U.S. assistant secretary of war. (loc)

As Sedgwick's division pushed west, with Sumner himself joining them, over 5,000 Federals were in three separate lines, one for each brigade. In front was Brig. Gen. Willis Gorman's command, followed by the brigades of Brig. Gen. N. J. T. Dana and Brig. Gen. Oliver Howard. All three brigades were composed of veterans, and their commanders were battle tested as well.

While marching westward, Sedgwick's men were passing the carnage of the morning's fight. Soldiers took care not to step on the bodies of the dead and dying, which literally covered the ground. Private Roland Bowen of the 15th Massachusetts, in the first line of the Federal advance, recalled in a letter home, "The field was strewn with dead men where Hooker had fought before us. One reb held up his hand and waved it as if to say, don't hurt me. As I steped [sic] over him said I, no one will hurt you."

When the Federals reached the Hagerstown Pike and began to climb over the fence alongside it, Confederate artillery fire peppered their ranks.

Maj. Gen. Lafayette McLaws's men crossed the Potomac in the early morning hours of September 17. Their attack in the West Woods devastated Sedgwick's division of the II Corps. (loc)

Capt. Oliver Wendell Holmes, Jr., of the 20th Massachusetts—and future associate justice of the Supreme Court of the United States—was wounded in the fighting in the West Woods. (loc)

Having fallen back from Nicodemus Heights due to the pressure exerted by the I Corps, the Confederate guns were now arrayed on Hauser Ridge and Reel Ridge, west and south of the West Woods. The guns were once again in a perfect position to stop and repulse a major Federal advance. Despite this harassing fire, Sedgwick's three brigades crossed the Pike and entered the West Woods.

Sedgwick's troops were not the first Federals to enter the woods that morning. In fact, there were already Union troops in the woodlot when the first of Sedgwick's men entered. To Sedgwick's left, behind the Dunker Church, the men of the 125th Pennsylvania, a brand new regiment which had just been formed that summer, had taken up a key position. As part of Crawford's brigade of the XII Corps, the 125th Pennsylvania was deployed near the East Woods earlier when they were ordered forward. Under the command of Col. Jacob Higgins, the rookie Pennsylvanians marched south along the Smoketown Road, pushing beyond the Hagerstown Pike and passing the Dunker Church. At more than 700 men strong, some observers thought an entire Union brigade was making the advance. Upon entering the woods, the Pennsylvanians encountered some skirmishers and remnants of Jackson's command from the earlier fighting. The green troops did not realize that they had taken a position far in advance of the rest of the army and that they were about to be punished severely for it.

It was at this moment that Lee's reinforcements, gathered from his right flank and from his reserve in Sharpsburg, were moving northward and preparing to enter the fight just a few hundred yards south of the Dunker Church. The men of Sedgwick's division and the newly reinforced Confederate left flank were on a collision course in the West Woods, one that would prove to be the bloodiest half-hour of the battle.

The first contact came against the ill-fated 125th Pennsylvania, precariously positioned behind the Dunker Church. As the Pennsylvanians were engaged in a firefight with the remnants of Jackson's earlier West Woods defense, they were hit from several angles by the advancing Confederates. The Virginians of Jubal Early's command, South Carolinians from Joseph Kershaw's brigade, and Mississippians led by William Barksdale all swarmed through the woods around the 125th Pennsylvania.

The Pennsylvanians had been joined by the 34th New York, one of Sedgwick's regiments which broke off from the main line and drifted south, but they too were quickly swept up in the Confederate tidal wave. When the 125th Pennsylvania and 34th New York gave way, Sedgwick's division was left completely exposed.

Color Sgt. George Simpson was killed soon after the 125th Pennsylvania was hit by Confederate infantry from McLaws's division. The statue of a color sergeant atop the 125th Pennsylvania memorial is in his honor. (ob)

As the sounds of battle grew into a steady roar, Edwin Sumner knew something had gone wrong. His three lines of battle were entangled in the woods, and they were too close to one another to execute any sort of organized turn to face this emerging threat. Gorman's men were engaged to their front with Confederate artillery and the men of Paul Semmes's brigade, while the rest of McLaws's division struck from the south. Chaos erupted. In some instances, Union regiments were firing into their own men when trying to stop the Confederate advance. As a veteran in the 19th Massachusetts later recalled, the scene was one "where Death was holding high revel."

In the midst of the fight, Sumner rode back through Sedgwick's lines, shouting at the top of his voice, "Back boys, for God's sake move back; you are in a bad fix!" In a letter home to his wife three days later, Sumner noted, "The enemy fought like maniacs to give you an idea of it. . . . I think I was never in such a fire as when that division broke—I was obliged to shout in such a way that I could not speak loud for some time afterwards."

In the third line, Oliver Howard desperately tried to turn his brigade, but found the task too daunting. As he gave the order to turn and face the attack, many of his men began to break for the rear. Amidst the roar of battle, pieces of various regiments tried to gather and make a stand north of the West Woods, including parts of the 1st Minnesota, 15th Massachusetts and the 106th Pennsylvania. While they attempted to hold their ground, these troops were overpowered by the Confederate onslaught and forced to retire toward the rear.

Alfred Waud captured the Confederate attack in the West Woods. (loc)

With Federals retreating in droves, Sedgwick's command had been virtually destroyed. The largest, most experienced division in the Union army had marched in three successive battle lines into the mouth of a violent Confederate attack, falling prey to yet another brilliant maneuver by Robert E. Lee. Lee did not necessarily plan this surprise counterattack, but his men happened to arrive at the right place and the right time. Sedgwick's division lost 2,228 men, the highest losses of any division at Antietam. For perspective, the three divisions of Hooker's I Corps combined had lost just a few hundred casualties more during the entire Cornfield fight, which lasted for three hours. Sedgwick's fight barely lasted a half hour.

In the front rank of Gorman's line, the 15th Massachusetts sustained the highest loss for any individual regiment at Antietam, losing 318 of its 606 men. Among those casualties was Pvt. Frank Bullard, who was struck by a piece of an artillery shell on his right thigh. Writing home several weeks later, Bullard recalled:

Brig. Gen. William Barksdale had been a political firebrand and ardent secessionist before the war. (loc)

The bullets came whizzing by my face, cutting down right and left, poor fellows falling thick and fast around me. You cannot realize the horrors of a battlefield, to see the dead and wounded, some with arms and legs off, cut up in every conceivable way. It was awful. The 15th regiment is now a mere corporal guard to what it was before the battle.

Not far behind Bullard and the 15th Massachusetts, Brig. Gen. N. J. T. Dana's brigade lost more than 800 men, the highest numerical loss for any Federal brigade at Antietam, prompting one officer to note, "my men fell around me like dead flies on a frosty morning." Among Dana's brigade was Dr. Edward Revere of the 20th Massachusetts, who went forward into battle with the regiment, led by his brother,

Lt. Col. Paul Revere. The Revere brothers were descendants of the famed hero of the Revolution and Boston silversmith, Paul Revere. In the chaos of the West Woods, Edward Revere was killed in action. Nine months later, his brother Paul was mortally wounded at Gettysburg.

Starke Avenue was named for Confederate Brig. Gen. William Starke, who was killed in this vicinity within the first hour of the battle. (cb)

In the wake of Sedgwick's repulse, parts of George Gordon's brigade of the XII Corps attempted to stop the Confederate advance. Two regiments—the 2nd Massachusetts and 13th New Jersey—rushed forward from the East Woods. When the Federals reached the Hagerstown Pike, Confederates blazed away into their ranks from the shelter of a rock ledge that had changed hands repeatedly throughout that morning. The fire was heavy enough to stop the regiments in their tracks, preventing them from stemming the Confederate tide.

Among those who were struck down at the fence was Lt. Col. Wilder Dwight of the 2nd Massachusetts. Several hours earlier, before going into battle, Dwight had begun writing a letter home to his mother. He was only halfway

Active throughout the morning of September 17, Brig. Gen. Jubal Early's brigade was one of many Confederate units that repulsed the II Corps in the West Woods. (loc)

The statue high atop the New Jersey Monument represents Capt. Hugh Irish of the 13th New Jersey who was killed near this spot after the repulse of Sedgwick's division. (cb)

The New Jersey Monument stands along the Hagerstown Pike near the spot where the 13th New Jersey and 2nd Massachusetts were sent forward to help stop the Confederate onslaught in the West Woods. (cb)

through when he was forced to pause and move forward with his command. Now, lying wounded in the left hip along the Hagerstown Pike, Dwight found time to finish his note home. Pulling out the half-written letter, Dwight took what time he had to pass along his goodbye to his family:

> *Dearest mother, I am wounded so as to be helpless. Good bye if so it must be I think I die in victory. God defend our country. I trust in God and love you all to the last. Dearest love to father and all my dear brothers. Our troops have left the part of the field where I lay—Mother, yours, Wilder.*

Dwight concluded by noting, "All is well with those that have faith." He died from his wounds two days later.

While the men of Gordon's brigade were unsuccessful in pushing back the Confederate advance, to the south the men of George Greene's division achieved noticeably greater success. Having taken the ground east of the Dunker Church earlier that morning, two of Greene's three brigades—those of Henry Stainrook and Hector Tyndale—were still in place when Sedgwick's division was driven from the woods.

At 10:00 a.m., Greene pushed his two brigades forward into the West Woods, encountering a second wave of advancing Confederates from John Walker's division. Greene's Federals were supported by II Corps artillery, and when they became engaged with Colonel Van Manning's brigade and parts of Kershaw's command, they succeeded in sweeping back the Confederate presence. Soon, Greene had pushed beyond the Dunker Church.

While Greene's gain was a major success, he lacked the men or resources to capitalize on it.

Rather than using his position to drive farther south and west, Greene had to contend with the remnants of the Confederate assault in the West Woods, as well as Confederate artillery on Hauser Ridge and Reel Ridge. Despite these obstacles, Greene managed to hold this ground for over two hours before he was pushed back to the eastern side of the Pike. Around noon, Greene's men were hit on both sides by two different Confederate brigades, forcing an urgent retreat back to the East Woods, where their day had begun several hours before.

Ever since the Iron Brigade's advance along the Hagerstown Pike shortly after 6:00 a.m., Union soldiers had been trying to establish a foothold in the West Woods. Now, with Greene's retreat, Confederates had driven the Army of the Potomac from the West Woods for the final time that day.

The 15th Massachusetts had the highest number of casualties for any single regiment in the battle. Their monument was dedicated in the West Woods on September 17, 1900. (cb)

By 10:00 a.m., over half of Antietam's casualties had fallen on the fields north of the Dunker Church. The Cornfield, West Woods, and their surrounding fields were littered with over 13,000 killed, wounded, or missing in action. Yet the bloodshed was far from over. Even before the guns had cooled in the West Woods, the rest of Sumner's II Corps was walking into a bloody fight along an old country lane just a short distance away.

Lt. Colonel Wilder Dwight of the 2nd Massachusetts finished a letter home to his family while lying mortally wounded in the hip near the Hagerstown Pike. (loc)

At the West Woods

A paved path from the West Woods parking area leads down to a small granite marker topped by the state seal of Maryland. It's one of a set of six monuments installed by Maryland across the battlefield on May 30, 1900. (cm)

The Confederate Baltimore Battery fired from the West Woods toward the Federal position in the Cornfield. A War Department marker points out that the battery included a 12-pounder iron howitzer, "the only one of its kind among the 500 cannon at Antietam." (cm)

The fields surrounding the parking area are known as Philadelphia Brigade Park. The Philadelphia Brigade monument itself was the result of veterans of the brigade—the 69th, 71st, 72nd, and 106th Pennsylvania—contacting Antietam Battlefield Board President Maj. George B. Davis in 1895 about placing monuments on the field at Antietam, which had been designated a National Battlefield by Congress just five years before. The veterans of the Philadelphia Brigade Association purchased 11 acres of property and placed one monument representing all four regiments of the brigade. The brigade's monument—the tallest on the battlefield today— was dedicated on September 17, 1896. In 1903, the city of Philadelphia took control of the park and monument and held it until it was transferred to the National Park Service in 1940.

Take some time to explore Philadelphia Brigade Park and the surrounding West Woods. Today, the woodlot is prospering thanks to reforestation efforts by the National Park Service over the course of the past 30 years. The West Woods trail runs through the woodlot, and follows the lines of Sedgwick's division. It begins behind the Dunker Church, next to the monuments for the 125th Pennsylvania and the 34th New York. Several War Department tablets mark the Confederate advance there as well.

The Philadelphia Brigade monument in the West Woods stands 73 feet tall. (cm)

➤ TO STOP 5

From the parking area, return to Dunker Church Road and turn right. In 0.2 miles turn left onto Smoketown Road. Continue 0.2 miles, and turn right onto Mumma Farm Lane. In 0.6 miles, turn left onto Richardson Avenue. The main parking lot for the Sunken Road tour stop is 0.2 miles ahead on your left. Note: additional parking can be found at the Observation Tower, which is 0.2 miles farther on your left.

GPS: N 39.47071 W 77.73978

The Fight for Bloody Lane

CHAPTER SEVEN

SEPTEMBER 17, 1862—9:30 A.M. TO 1 P.M.

As the battle raged in the Cornfield that morning, the sounds of war spread across the rest of the landscape surrounding the peaceful town of Sharpsburg. Just over a mile south of the Cornfield, the echoes of cannon shot and musketry dipped into an old sunken road, worn down by years of wagon use. Previously it had only been known to local families, such as the Pipers, Mummas, and Roulettes. Soon, it was to be forever known as Bloody Lane.

This Sunken Road was the focal point of Confederate Gen. Daniel Harvey Hill's division. While Hill's command consisted of five brigades, three of them had been sent into the Cornfield earlier that morning, leaving only the Alabamians of Brig. Gen. Robert Rodes and the North Carolinians of Brig. Gen. George B. Anderson left to hold the line, over 2,000 men total. Rodes and Anderson had originally been posted south of the road, and had just moved north toward the position when they found themselves at the center of a major fight that was erupting.

As John Sedgwick's division of the Federal II Corps was being mauled in the West Woods, Maj. Gen. William French's division was arriving on the field near the East Woods. Known as "Old Blinky," French was a veteran officer with a long career

Antietam's "Bloody Lane" is one of the most iconic landscapes of the Civil War. (cb)

before the Civil War. His division at Antietam, however, was anything but battle tested. Only three of his 10 regiments had any combat experience.

Upon reaching the East Woods that morning, French received orders from Sumner informing him of the positions of Sedgwick and Greene. The former had pushed into the West Woods, while the latter held ground west of the now-burning Mumma farmstead, where Confederates were gathering beyond Greene's left flank.

This photo looks west across the battlefield from the base of Antietam's observation tower. (cb)

While Sumner had intended on keeping French to the left of Sedgwick, a more pressing need meant that now he was to advance to Greene's left, passing the Mumma farm and meeting the new threat to the south. Thus, French turned his division southward, a decision which put him on a collision course with D. H. Hill's command in the Sunken Road.

The Sunken Road had both benefits and drawbacks as a defensive line. It served as a ready-made trench for the Southern troops who would hold it. The terrain around the road rises to a ridge some 70 to 100 yards in front of where the Confederate line was located, dropping away and running down toward the Roulette farm beyond the ridge. Thus, by the time Federal soldiers had reached the ridge and could see the Southern troops, they were well within range of the Confederates, many of whom had smoothbore muskets. Additionally, the Confederate position was strengthened by considerable artillery power. Just south of the Sunken Road lay the Piper farm. The ridges on this farm, and beyond it on the Reel farm, provided a significant platform for Southern artillery to blast the advancing Federals trying to break the Confederate center.

Maj. Gen. William "Blinky" French's II Corps division was the first to attack Confederates in the Sunken Road. (loc)

Of course, while the terrain did provide some advantages, its biggest drawback was that it was a low point, affording the enemy the opportunity to fire down at a sheltered opponent should Federal soldiers seize the ridges overlooking the road.

Among the Southerners in the road was John Brown Gordon, the colonel of the 6th Alabama. Gordon and his men had not been in the Sunken Road long before the sights and sounds of the advancing enemy reached them. "The banners above them had apparently never been discolored by the smoke and dust of battle," Gordon remembered. "Their gleaming bayonets flashed like burnished silver in the sunlight. With the precision of step and perfect alignment of a holiday parade, this magnificent array moved to the charge. . . . As we stood looking upon that brilliant pageant, I thought, if I did not say, 'What a pity to spoil with bullets such a scene of martial beauty.'" When the Federal ranks closed in on Gordon's line, a blast of musket fire erupted, tearing apart the attacking troops. "The effect was appalling," Gordon wrote. "The entire front line, with few exceptions went down in the consuming blast."

A monument for the 132nd Pennsylvania stands in the Sunken Road. (cb)

The front line of the Federal assault consisted of Brig. Gen. Max Weber's brigade, troops experiencing their trial by fire that morning. In the first 15 minutes of their attack on the Sunken Road, over 400 men were shot down in front of the Confederate lines. In the 1st Delaware, the losses were especially egregious, as eight of the 10 company commanders were hit.

With their initial attack repulsed, the Federals scattered back to regroup and try again. Among the Delawareans, 2nd Lt. Charles Tanner noticed that the regimental flag had been left behind amidst the casualties in front of the enemy line. With the help of soldiers from the 5th Maryland, the 1st Delaware laid down a heavy fire on the road and tried several times to reclaim its fallen flag. "Maddened and more desperate than ever," Tanner recalled, "I called for the men to make another effort." Rushing forward once more, Tanner reached the colors, just yards in front of the Confederates, when he was struck in the arm. Seizing the flag, he turned and ran for the rear, being hit twice more by Confederate fire in the process. For saving the flag of the 1st Delaware, Tanner was promoted to 1st Lieutenant and became one of the 20 men who would earn the Medal of Honor for their actions at Antietam that day.

With Confederates falling rapidly, the Federal attack did not abate. After Weber's severe losses, Col. Dwight Morris's men were next to attack the Sunken Road. Morris's line was not more than 200 yards behind Weber's, and when the front ranks broke apart from heavy losses, Morris's men pushed forward into the Confederate fire. Coming up to support him was Brig. Gen. Nathan

The charge by the Irish Brigade is captured in bronze bas-relief on a monument near the south end of the Sunken Road. Dedicated in October 1997, the monument was sculpted by Ron Tunison. (cm)

Kimball's command, composed primarily of veteran troops. Kimball's line advanced on both sides of the Roulette farm lane, which ran northwest from the Sunken Road, connecting it to the Clipp House and William Roulette's farm beyond it.

Though his family was Irish through and through, Thomas Galwey was born in London and came to the United States with his parents at the age of five, settling near Cleveland, Ohio. He was 16 years old and serving in the 8th Ohio on the morning of September 17. In his postwar writings, Galwey remembered kneeling in the grass and firing into the Confederate lines as the battle raged. All around him, Galwey saw death and suffering. Nearby, Lt. John Lantry, who had emigrated from Canada as a young boy with his family, was struck in the head by an artillery shell and killed in brutal fashion. Galwey later recalled the scene:

Brig. Gen. Thomas Francis Meagher looks out in 3-D from the Irish Brigade monument—the unit he raised and then commanded until early 1863. (cm)

The din is frightful. Alas, no words can depict the horrors of a great battle as they appear to men accustomed to them. We had seen a great deal of service before now; but our fighting had been mostly of

Samuel and Elizabeth Mumma fled their farm with their 10 kids before the battle. The photograph (top) and painting (right) show the Mumma farm before and during the fight. Confederates torched the farm—the only intentional act of property destruction during the battle. The Mumma family rebuilt their farm in 1863. It still stands on Antietam National Battlefield (left). (loc)(cb)(loc)

the desultory, skirmishing sort. What we see now looks to us like systematic killing.

In the 14th Indiana, Lt. Augustus Van Dyke noted that the incoming Confederate artillery fire caused moments of unimaginable carnage all around him. "Death from the bullet is ghastly," Van Dyke wrote, "but to see a man's brains dashed out at our side by a grape shot and another's body severed by a screeching cannon ball is truly appalling. May I never again see such horrors as I saw that day."

With Confederate musket fire pouring out of the Sunken Road, punctuated only by the concussions of artillery shells exploding in the air, raining shrapnel down upon the men, the scene was beyond description for many who witnessed it. One New Yorker wrote that it was "a savage

Pictured here as a general later in the war, John Gordon was a colonel commanding the 6th Alabama when he was wounded five times in the fight for the Sunken Road. Before the war, Gordon was an attorney in Georgia, and when the conflict began, he organized a company known as the "Raccoon Roughs," which became part of the 6th Alabama. (loc)

The 8th Ohio suffered 49 percent casualties in assaulting the Sunken Road. Their monument was dedicated in 1903. (cb)

continual thunder that I cannot compare to any sound I ever heard."

In the Sunken Road itself, Confederates had their own harrowing experiences. Colonel Gordon of the 6th Alabama was among those hit numerous times, receiving two wounds in his right leg, one in his left arm, and another in his left shoulder. While Gordon remained on the field, a fifth bullet hit him on the left side of his face and exited through his neck. Gordon fell to the ground bleeding profusely, lying with his face in his own hat. As he later wrote, "it would seem that I might have been smothered by the blood running into my cap from this last wound but for the act of some Yankee, who, as if to save my life, had at a previous hour during the battle, shot a hole through the cap, which let the blood run out." With Gordon lying unconscious in the road, command of his regiment fell to Lt. Col. James Lightfoot.

As the Confederates struggled to keep up the fight, help was arriving from the division of Maj. Gen. Richard H. Anderson, which rushed through the Piper farm fields to join what remained of D. H. Hill's division in the road. Approaching the field, Anderson was badly wounded, as were several of his brigade commanders, further depriving the Confederates of experienced leaders. With reinforcements arriving, the Southerners made several attempts to attack out from the Sunken Road toward the Federals, but to little avail.

While the Confederates fought valiantly, they could not hold their position forever. By 10:30 a.m., Maj. Gen. Israel Richardson's Federal division arrived. Richardson's veteran soldiers were the final II Corps division to reach the field, having been held in reserve until Maj. Gen. George Morrell's division of the V Corps arrived to take their place.

Leading the division's advance was Brig. Gen. Thomas Francis Meagher's brigade, which would become one of the most famous brigades of the Civil War—known today simply as the Irish Brigade. At Antietam, the brigade consisted of three Irish regiments from New York, as well as the 29th

Massachusetts, whose men were largely descended from English settlers around Boston. Despite this clash of cultures, their commander was distinctively Irish. Brigadier General Meagher had been an Irish revolutionary who was imprisoned, escaped to the United States, and became a prominent figure in New York City before the war.

As Meagher's men advanced toward the Sunken Road that morning, "the shot and shell of the enemy poured over our heads," recalled Lt. James Turner, a member of the general's staff. When they closed in on the Confederate line, the two sides blazed away at each other with blistering volleys of musket fire. Several of Meagher's regiments tried to push forward to the road itself, but sustained such heavy losses they were unable to reach the Confederate position. Holding the ridge in front of the Confederate line, Meagher's men continued to fire into the Southern ranks as their casualties mounted. In the course of the fight, Meagher's entire staff became casualties; even the general himself was thrown to the ground when his horse was severely wounded.

In the Confederate lines, casualties were continuing to mount as well. On the right, brigade commander George B. Anderson was struck in the ankle, a wound that would prove mortal when it later became infected. The brigade's second in command, Col. Charles Courtenay Tew of the 2nd North Carolina, was soon notified he was in command. Tew had the distinction of being the first honor graduate of the first graduating class from the South Carolina Military Academy in Charleston, known as the Citadel. No sooner had he taken command than Tew was mortally wounded by a ball passing through his temple. Elsewhere along the line, Confederates were suffering heavily. Every officer in the 4th North Carolina was killed or wounded during the fight.

As the Irish Brigade ran low on ammunition on the ridges in front of the road, a fifth attacking brigade rushed to their assistance, this one commanded by Brig. Gen. John Caldwell. While Meagher's lines melted away, Caldwell's men rushed up to their ranks and provided a decisive blow against the

Pvt. Samuel Cole Wright, Company E of the 29th Massachusetts. During the advance of the Irish Brigade on the Sunken Road, the 19-year-old private volunteered to help take down a fence that blocked the Federals' path. He was wounded in the process, and was later awarded the Medal of Honor. Wright was wounded several more times during the war, including one injury that destroyed his right eye. He survived the war and lived until 1906. (loc)

A mortuary cannon marks where Confederate Brig. Gen. George B. Anderson was mortally wounded. (cb)

Just south of the Sunken Road, the Piper farm saw Confederates both advancing to and retreating from the Confederate lines during the brutal fight for the road. (cb)

Maj. Gen. Israel Richardson commanded the 1st division of the II Corps. A member of the West Point class of 1841, Richardson served with gallantry in the Mexican War and took up farming in Michigan in the mid-1850s. When the Civil War began, he recruited the 2nd Michigan, and he led a brigade at First Manassas in 1861. (loc)

Confederates in the Sunken Road. Several of Caldwell's regiments surged forward, breaking into the Confederate line at last.

With heavy fire now pouring down on the Confederates from multiple angles, the Sunken Road became an untenable position. Richard Anderson's command, as well as parts of George B. Anderson's North Carolina brigade, began streaming out of the road toward the rear. With their right weakened, Rodes's Alabamians were threatened both on their front and their flank. Orders were given to Lieutenant Colonel Lightfoot of the 6th Alabama to turn his flank to protect it from the enfilading fire. Instead of altering his position, however, Lightfoot misheard the order and commanded his men to retreat from the road altogether. With Confederates fleeing from all parts of the line, the Sunken Road position had finally fallen.

On the hills and fields of the Piper farm to the south, chaos was reigning. Wounded generals and soldiers alike intermingled, with the officers attempting to form a new defensive line amidst the remnants of the fallen Confederate center. It was all hands on deck for the Southern troops, with officers such as D. H. Hill and James Longstreet taking part in the fight. Longstreet was seen in the Piper orchard, calmly holding the reins of his staff officers' horses while they loaded and fired an artillery piece against the Federal lines.

However, in this moment of apparent breakthrough and opportunity for the Federals, confusion, counterattacks, and artillery fire prevented any further gains. Five Federal brigades had taken part in the Sunken Road fight, leaving many of their number now dead or wounded upon the fields around the Confederate lines. Only Col. John Brooke's brigade of Richardson's division had not been engaged, and one fresh brigade was not enough to storm the Piper farm and capitalize on the Union success.

Despite the fall of the Sunken Road, Confederates

Brig. Gen. Ambrose Wright was wounded as his men reinforced the Sunken Road position. (loc)

Following the mortal wounding of Israel Richardson, Brig. Gen. Winfield Scott Hancock assumed command of Richardson's division. (loc)

Lt. Col. Nelson Miles took command of the 61st and 64th New York when their commander, Col. Francis Barlow, was wounded on September 17. He later went on to earn the Medal of Honor at Chancellorsville and became a major general by the end of the Civil War. In 1895, he became the Commanding General of the U.S. Army and led the army during the Spanish-American War. (loc)

were not done fighting on this part of the field. Once the remnants of Richardson's command were passing through the Sunken Road, a Confederate counterattack struck Greene's men in the West Woods, driving them from the position there once and for all. Confederates of John Walker's division pushed past Greene's command and attacked into the right flank of French's exhausted men, forcing several brigades to turn and defend their flank rather than press forward toward the Piper farm.

Making matters worse, D. H. Hill gathered enough men to launch two counterattacks toward the left flank of the Union line along the Sunken Road, supported by heavy canister fire from the Washington Artillery, located in the Piper orchard. Hill's attacks helped to halt the Federal advance, and with the heavy artillery fire coming from the Piper farm behind them, the Federals who pushed south from the Sunken Road were overwhelmed—their ranks torn apart by canister and shells.

Recognizing that his attack had reached a critical point, Richardson ordered his men back to the Sunken Road and searched for any Federal artillery that could be brought forward to support his position. While he was trying to steady his lines, however, an exploding artillery shell struck Richardson in the shoulder, mortally wounding

A mortuary cannon indicates the area where Israel Richardson was mortally wounded by Confederate artillery fire. (cb)

In the aftermath of the fighting, a Northern correspondent noted that the Confederate dead "were lying in rows like the ties of a railroad, in heaps, like cord-wood mingled with the splintered and shattered fence rails. Words are inadequate to portray the scene." (loc)

him. For all of his promise, experience, and ability, "Fighting Dick" Richardson lingered for several months, dying from his wound that November.

With casualties mounting, Confederate shells and confusion saw the tide of Union momentum ebb and collapse. By 1:00 p.m., the Federal assault on the Sunken Road had come to a merciful end. As they had done on the northern end of the field that morning against Lee's left, yet again Union soldiers had driven the Confederates back, gaining much ground, but were ultimately unable to deliver the crushing blow that would have sent the gray lines reeling. Between the two sides, over 5,500 more casualties had been added to Antietam's ghastly toll. Because of these losses, the Sunken Road has since been known as Bloody Lane.

By the time fighting had ceased along this part of the line, it had been just over seven hours since the first rays of dawn broke across the battlefield. In that time nearly 60,000 soldiers in blue and gray had been sent into battle north of Sharpsburg. Roughly 19,000 of them had been killed, wounded, or were missing in action.

At the Sunken Road

From the parking lot, the Sunken Road is just to your front. A short trail takes you down into the road itself, which is a must-see for any Antietam visitor. From there, you can either walk down the Roulette farm lane towards the Roulette farm, or you can pick up the 1.5 mile Bloody Lane trail, which is accessible from several locations along the road.

Looking to the southeast, the War Department Observation Tower is visible. Built in 1897, the tower is a reminder of the park's early history, when it was one of the first Civil War battlefields to be protected by the War Department. The War Department managed limited holdings at Antietam until 1933, when Antietam was turned over to the National Park Service, along with the other Civil War battlefields the War Department was administering. From the top of the tower, nearly the entire battlefield is visible. The view makes climbing the 71 steps worthwhile.

▶ **TO STOP 6**

Continue 0.8 miles to the intersection with state route 34. After the stop sign, proceed straight across onto Rodman Avenue. In 0.6 miles, turn left onto Branch Avenue. Proceed 0.5 miles to the Burnside Bridge parking lot. There is a pathway going down the hill from the parking area to the bridge. It is accessible from the NPS overlook, as well as near the McKinley monument. Overflow parking can be found in the large field south of the parking area. The Final Attack Trail and Snavely's Ford Trail both start at this parking area.

Looking northwest across the battlefield from the Observation Tower today (top) and in 1953 (bottom). Among the notable differences from the modern landscape, note the souvenir stand along the Sunken Road, and the vacant hillside behind it where the Visitor Center currently sits. Other visible landmarks include the New York monument in the distance. (cm)(nps)

GPS: N 39.44973 W 77.73268

Burnside Bridge

CHAPTER EIGHT

SEPTEMBER 17, 1862—9 A.M. TO 1 P.M.

Throughout the morning of September 17, the battle of Antietam resembled an aggressive game of chess for Robert E. Lee. When George McClellan launched attacks against the Confederate left flank, Lee countered by drawing troops from other parts of the field to prevent a debilitating breakthrough on the Confederate line. However, in stymieing each of these assaults, Lee had been gradually weakening his right to strengthen his left, so much so that by noon there was only one Confederate division south of Sharpsburg. Brigadier General David Rumph Jones's small division of some 2,500 men was now to be the sole defender of Lee's right flank.

A member of the famed West Point Class of 1846, Jones was an experienced officer who had served in the War with Mexico. At Antietam, Jones had six brigades under his command, including those of Robert Toombs, G. T. Anderson, Thomas Drayton, James Kemper, Micah Jenkins, and Richard Garnett. Having already lost Anderson's brigade, which was sent to the West Woods that morning, Jones had to be sensible with how he deployed the rest of his men. The terrain they had to defend was vast, stretching for several miles south of Sharpsburg, punctuated by several steep ridges and ravines that ran in between the town and

The sycamore tree at the far end of Burnside Bridge is a witness tree—one there at the time of battle. (cm)

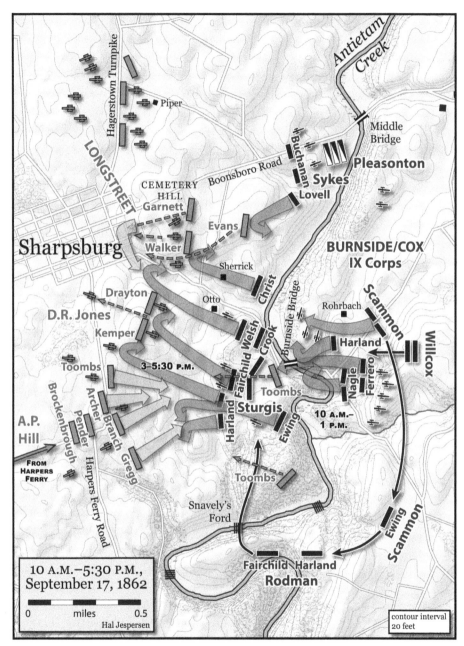

10 A.M.-5:30 P.M. SEPTEMBER 17, 1862—The southern phase of Antietam got underway around mid-morning on the 17th when the IX Corps began its assaults against the lower bridge. Although they were across the creek by 1 p.m., it took until mid-afternoon before the Federal assault finally launched against Lee's right flank. By the time the IX Corps was closing in on Sharpsburg, Confederate reinforcements from Gen. A. P. Hill's division arrived, driving back the Federal flank and ending the Union assault.

Antietam Creek. One of the key crossing points over that creek—the Lower Bridge—was directly in

Lush growth now covers the western bank of Antietam Creek. (cm)

front of Jones's line. The Confederates realized this bridge was a crucial point on the creek and was one that needed to be defended, a task that fell to Brig. Gen. Robert Toombs's brigade.

Toombs selected Col. Henry Benning and two regiments—the 2nd and 20th Georgia—to defend the bridge itself. When the Georgians moved forward to Antietam Creek, they were on steep hills nearly 80 feet high looking down on a narrow bridge, not more than 12 feet wide. Because of the inaccessible banks of the creek, there were no easily found fording sites nearby, making the bridge an essential feature for any units hoping to cross the Antietam on the southern half of the battlefield. To defend the bridge, Benning's men stacked up fence rails where they could form "rude barricades," as Benning wrote. Where no fence rails were found, the men simply used the slope of the ground and surrounding trees, all of which formed a natural defensive line. Once again, Confederate troops were well positioned to take advantage of all that the terrain around Sharpsburg had to offer.

While Jones's men had terrain on their side, they had little else. At the start of the day, John Walker's division had been positioned on Jones's right, guarding Snavely's Ford across the Antietam. However, when Lee ordered Walker north toward the West Woods that morning, Snavely's Ford was left unguarded, and the Confederate flank was exposed.

Col. Henry L. Benning commanded the Confederate defenders of Burnside Bridge. Benning was an attorney and justice of the Georgia Supreme Court before the Civil War and an ardent supporter of secession. He became a brigadier general in the Confederate army in 1863. (loc)

Maj. Gen. Ambrose Burnside maintained his status as a wing commander in the Army of the Potomac, overseeing the Federal attacks on the southern end of the field. (loc)

*　*　*

On the eastern side of the Antietam, the Union IX Corps awoke on September 17 to face arguably the toughest challenge of any Union command at the battle that day. With four divisions and more than 12,000 men, the problems affecting the corps did not deal as much with strength as with experience. It was an entirely new command, built earlier in September from divisions who had not fought together before. In fact, all four division commanders in the corps assumed their post in September 1862.

At South Mountain on the 14th, the IX Corps was led by Maj. Gen. Jesse Reno, who was killed at Fox's Gap. Now, the corps was led by Brig. Gen. Jacob Cox, but with a wrinkle. During the advance from Washington, McClellan had placed the I Corps and IX Corps together under the leadership of Maj. Gen. Ambrose Burnside. Once at Antietam, however, the two commands were split up and sent to opposite ends of the field. Despite this, Burnside believed he was still operating as a wing commander, and remained with the IX Corps in the field. As a result, the IX Corps effectively had two commanders at Antietam: Ambrose Burnside, its wing commander, and Jacob Cox, its direct commander. Because Burnside was Cox's superior, he was still in overall command.

Also known as the Lower Bridge or Rohrbach Bridge, this view of Burnside Bridge was taken by Alexander Gardner, looking north toward the bridge from the eastern side of Antietam Creek in September 1862. (loc)

Complicating matters further, the IX Corps was almost entirely on its own on the Union left flank. On the Union right, the fighting around the Cornfield, West Woods, and Sunken Road saw troops from four different army corps involved throughout the day. To the south, the IX Corps had only a few regiments from the V Corps offering assistance.

As McClellan had envisioned it, once the battle was a few hours old and Lee's strength and intentions had been discovered, Burnside was to send his men across the Antietam to strike the Confederate right flank, possibly crushing it and severing Lee's escape back to Virginia. At 7:00 a.m., McClellan sent word for the IX Corps to be ready to move, yet the order to advance was not given until just after 9:00 a.m.

While the main objective was to strike the Confederate right flank near Sharpsburg, Burnside first had to get his command across the Antietam. With few places to ford the creek that day, the Lower Bridge—today known as the Burnside Bridge—was to be the focus of their efforts. The approach to the bridge did not allow for a large advance, and considering the bridge's narrow width, only a few regiments at a time could storm the position. Making this essential crossing point all the more difficult, Col. Henry Benning's Georgians were ready and waiting to stop the Federal advance.

Robert Toombs commanded a brigade of Confederates charged with defending the ground overlooking Burnside Bridge. Before the war, Toombs was a United States congressman and senator from Georgia, and served as the first Confederate Secretary of State at the outset of the conflict. (loc)

The first regiment to move against the bridge was the 11th Connecticut, led by the youthful Col. Henry Kingsbury. Kingsbury had graduated from West Point in May 1861, and, as one of his classmates said, "He embarked on a career which nothing but death could terminate in failure." The recently married colonel—his wife was a niece of Zachary Taylor and the sister-in-law of David R. Jones, with whom Kingsbury was good friends—was just 25 years old, and had just taken command of his regiment that summer.

Shortly after 10:00 a.m., Kingsbury led the 11th Connecticut forward against the Lower Bridge, advancing down the Rohrbach farm lane. Upon approaching the bridge, however, the Federals were caught by a fierce wave of Confederate fire pouring down on them. Captain John Griswold attempted to forge ahead by leading several companies into the creek, failing to reach the other side amidst a storm of Confederate bullets.

Brig. Gen. Jacob D. Cox assumed command of the IX Corps following Jesse Reno's death at South Mountain. After the war, he went on to become the governor of Ohio. (loc)

Griswold was among those hit, and if not for several of his men, he would have died in the waters of the Antietam. He was carried back to a field hospital by his men, where he instructed the surgeons to look to others instead of him. He died the following day. A Yale graduate who spoke three languages, Griswold left a deep impression on Ambrose Burnside, who visited the wounded captain before he died. Griswold reportedly told the general, "I die as I have ever wished to die, for my country."

While Griswold's men were stopped in the creek, Henry Kingsbury fared no better. Pinned down near the bridge itself, Kingsbury was struck four times by Confederate infantry fire. He, too, was carried back to a Union field hospital, dying on the 18th as well.

A popular Kurz and Allison lithograph shows the fight for Burnside Bridge. (loc)

Burnside visited Kingsbury on the night of the 17th, bidding a tearful goodbye to a young man whom he had mentored after his father's death in 1856. Indeed, Burnside was made the executor of Kingsbury's estate upon his passing. Kingsbury's widow, Eva, was pregnant with the couple's first child at the time. When he was born, Kingsbury's son was named for his late father.

With their officers struck down among their many enlisted men, the efforts of the 11th Connecticut were largely lost. The 11th was meant to be a heavy skirmish line, preparing for the advance of Col. George Crook's brigade of Ohioans. Unfortunately, Crook's command strayed to the north, ending up nowhere near the

Federals seize Burnside Bridge, as sketched by Edwin Forbes. (loc)

bridge they were ordered to take. With Crook's misdirection and Kingsbury's repulse, the first advance on the bridge had failed.

By 11:00 a.m., Brig. Gen. James Nagle's brigade launched a second attack on the bridge, using the 2nd Maryland and 6th New Hampshire. With the 2nd Maryland leading the way, Nagle's men were to advance from the south, hopefully being shielded from Confederate fire on the other side by the terrain along the creek. Lieutenant Colonel Jacob Duryee—whose father, Abram Duryee, had led his brigade through the cornfield that morning—

led his Marylanders along the creek, but was only able to get to about 200 yards away from the bridge before the heavy Confederate fire forced them back, along with the 6th New Hampshire. The rest of Nagle's brigade tried to provide covering fire, but it was of little use. The second attack on the bridge failed as well.

While this fighting was going on, Burnside and Cox were frustrated not just by the lack of success against the bridge but by the actions of Brig. Gen. Isaac Rodman's division. Not wanting to rely solely on the Lower Bridge as a crossing point, Rodman's command was sent south to find a ford across the creek. Unfortunately for Rodman, and luckily for the Confederates, it took several hours to find Snavely's Ford, which was significantly farther south of where Union staff officers had thought it to be, costing valuable time for the Federals.

A plaque on the Maryland Monument depicts the attack of the 2nd Maryland at Burnside Bridge. (cb)

As the hours passed with no progress at the bridge, McClellan had sent numerous staff officers to IX Corps headquarters, hoping to move things along. This served only to further irritate Burnside, who ordered yet another assault on the bridge, this one by Maj. Gen. Samuel Sturgis's division. Brigadier General Edward Ferrero chose the 51st Pennsylvania and 51st New York for the task, and addressed them before sending them into the fight. Ferrero reportedly promised the hard-drinking Pennsylvanians that their whiskey ration would be restored upon the successful completion of their orders.

At 12:30 p.m., with their desperation mounting, the New Yorkers and Pennsylvanians charged straight forward against the bridge, rushing downhill while the rest of Ferrero's brigade provided covering fire. The men took shelter behind the stone and wooden fences along the creek on either side of the bridge and sent a blistering counterfire against Benning's Georgians across the creek. In the heat of battle, the color bearers from each regiment rushed forward, followed by their officers and men, and

Brig. Gen. Edward Ferrero, who had been a dance instructor in New York before the war, oversaw the final attack against Burnside Bridge. (loc)

Future President William McKinley served as a quartermaster sergeant in the 23rd Ohio at Antietam. Though he did not see heavy combat at Antietam, this monument was erected to him in 1903, two years after he was assassinated while in office. The close-up shows McKinley as a solider and as a president.(cm)

by 1:00 p.m. Burnside had finally gotten his men across the bridge that now bears his name.

On top of the bluffs, Federals saw Benning's Georgians retreating in droves. Having been engaged for almost three hours, many of the men had run low on ammunition and had no choice but to fall back. Others retreated because Ferrero's men had wrested control of the bridge once and for all. Still others fell back because, to their south, Rodman's command had finally crossed the creek at Snavely's Ford, posing a grave threat to the Confederate flank. With all of these problems arising at once, Toombs's men gave way and headed back toward the remainder of Jones's division, where they would prepare for the final fight for the Confederate flank.

Though his men had finally gotten across the creek, the real task was just now beginning for Burnside and the IX Corps. They had taken the bridge, but they did not yet have nearly enough men to launch an attack on the Confederate line.

Thousands of reinforcements had to be brought forward across the creek, as well as ammunition and several artillery batteries, all of which would cost two hours of precious time that Burnside did not have.

Burnside sent word to McClellan's headquarters that he was across the creek at last, requesting reinforcements for his attack south of Sharpsburg. McClellan responded by sending Maj. Thomas Key back to Burnside with word that no help would be sent. While the VI Corps had recently arrived on the field, it was deployed in the East Woods to protect the shattered Federal right. McClellan had two divisions of the V Corps near the Middle Bridge, and part of Brig. Gen. George Sykes's command was on the western side of the creek. Sykes's left would advance alongside Burnside's men, but the rest of Sykes's division was needed to hold the ground near the Boonsboro Pike. For the final attack of the day, the IX Corps was to be almost entirely on its own.

Burnside Bridge was open to vehicle traffic well into the twentieth century. Note the monuments placed on the corners of the bridge itself. These were later moved to the path near the bridge. (loc)

At Burnside Bridge

Of all the misunderstood places at Antietam, Burnside Bridge is perhaps the most misunderstood. For generations, the prevailing interpretation held that the bridge was the scene of the "afternoon phase" of the battle, which featured the inept Ambrose Burnside foolishly trying to seize an irrelevant bridge rather than simply having his men wade through the waters of Antietam Creek. Indeed, Henry Kyd Douglass, a staff officer under Stonewall Jackson who hailed from nearby Shepherdstown, Virginia (today West Virginia), famously wrote of the bridge, "It was no pass of Thermopylae. Go look at it and tell me if you don't think Burnside and his corps might

Originally built in 1836, Burnside Bridge went through a massive restoration project in 2015 and 2016, ensuring it will remain standing for generations to come. (cm)

have executed a hop, skip, and jump and landed on the other side. One thing is certain, they may have waded it that day without getting their waist belts wet in any place."

While Douglass's words are certainly quotable, that does not make them true. Burnside had no choice but to take the bridge for several reasons. It was nearly impossible for regiments of soldiers to ford the Antietam near the site of Burnside Bridge that day. The water was not all that high and swift, but rather, the bottom of the creek was too filled with sand and sediment for men to get their footing, and the banks were too steep for soldiers to climb out, especially while under fire. Moreover, Burnside had 12,000 men under his command. Had he tried crossing them through the creek, a major traffic jam would have occurred. The bridge was a necessary objective for Burnside. Taking it cost him time, but he had no choice.

Additionally, the fighting around Burnside Bridge has often been described as the afternoon phase of the battle. Far from it: the fighting there took place mostly during the late morning hours of the 17th. By 1:00 p.m., the bridge had been taken, and Union soldiers were beginning to gather on the western side of the creek. Despite its fame, the Federals lost roughly 500 casualties in taking the bridge, meaning it was far from the bloodiest spot on the field that day.

From the parking area overlooking Antietam Creek, there is a walkway that takes visitors down to the bridge itself. If you choose to walk to the bridge, you will spot the famous Sycamore Witness Tree on the eastern bank of the Antietam on the northern side of the bridge. The hillside looking down on the bridge still bears evidence of the fighting there, as the rifle pits used by the Georgian defenders are still visible.

Near the parking lot, the William McKinley monument is also accessible. McKinley was a young commissary sergeant in the 23rd Ohio who brought forward coffee and rations to his men once they were engaged in battle on the western side of the Antietam. McKinley went on to become the 25th President of the United States. In 1903, two years after he was killed by an assassin's bullet, the state of Ohio erected this monument in McKinley's honor. McKinley died on September 14, 1901, on the 39th anniversary of the battle of South Mountain.

This parking area is also the starting point for several trails. The Final Attack Trail starts to your west, covering the battle action that will be discussed in the next chapter. The Snavely's Ford Trail also starts from here, beginning just south of the parking area. The Union Advance Trail begins from Burnside Bridge on the eastern side of Antietam Creek.

▶ **TO STOP 7**

Follow the tour road down the hillside from the parking lot, and continue 0.5 miles. At the stop sign, continue on Branch Avenue for 0.2 miles. The parking area is on your left.

GPS: N 39.45338 W 77.73923

The Final Attack

CHAPTER NINE

SEPTEMBER 17, 1862—LATE AFTERNOON

Captain Newton Manross of the 16th Connecticut was an example of the finest the Union army had to offer. A distinguished professor at Amherst College in Massachusetts when the war began, Manross was an expert geologist, having studied at Yale and received his doctorate at the University of Gottingen in Germany. Manross had been across the globe studying rock formations and natural gasses, making him one of the most distinguished soldiers in either army at Antietam. Despite his accolades and intellect, however, Captain Manross knew no limits on his patriotism.

In the summer of 1862, when Lincoln called for more volunteers to put down the rebellion, Manross was one of the hundreds of thousands who came forward, enlisting in the 16th Connecticut. To his dear wife at home, Manross conveyed his logic in a letter of July 22, noting, "you can better afford to have a country without a husband than a husband without a country." At age 37, Manross became the captain of Company K, 16th Connecticut. For all of his accomplishments, patriotism, and intellect, Captain Manross was to be caught up in the last, bloody crescendo of Antietam on the afternoon of September 17, 1862, along with thousands of others in the final attack of the Union army that day.

The Army of the Potomac launched its final attack at Antietam across these fields south of Sharpsburg. (cb)

*   *   *

When that fateful September day began, Maj. Gen. Ambrose Powell Hill's Confederate division was 17 miles south of Sharpsburg and still in Harpers Ferry. Following the Union surrender there on September 15, most of the Confederates who captured the town headed north to rejoin Lee and the main body of the army in Sharpsburg. Hill and his men were left behind to handle more than 12,000 Union prisoners and the captured goods, waiting to join Lee at a later time.

Hill's division was composed of veteran troops who had acquitted themselves well on several battlefields. Hill himself was a veteran commander, with First Manassas, Williamsburg, the Seven Days' battles, Cedar Mountain, and Second Manassas all on his resume by the time of Antietam. During the Maryland campaign, Hill's division was under Jackson's command and had proven itself of great worth during the operations around Harpers Ferry.

Early that morning, however, Hill received word from Sharpsburg that he was needed there and that the matter was urgent. His orders arrived at 6:30 a.m., when the fighting in the Cornfield was already more than 30 minutes old. Taking time to gather his division, Hill was on the road marching north from Harpers Ferry by 7:30 that morning, leaving only four Georgia regiments behind to deal with the thousands of Union prisoners. With Brig. Gen. Maxcy Gregg's South Carolinians in the lead, Hill's men embarked on one of the most famous marches of the Civil War. While the men marched north through Virginia, many noticed that their division commander was wearing the red flannel shirt that he typically donned on days of battle. The men kept a steady pace as they advanced, though the sunshine above and the miles ahead became too much for some of the soldiers who fell back and straggled from the ranks.

As Hill's men marched toward Boteler's Ford to cross the Potomac near Shepherdstown, Robert E. Lee was in Sharpsburg nervously trying to reinforce his center and his right. With fewer than 3,000 soldiers

Before the war, Maj. Gen. Ambrose Powell Hill had been engaged to marry Mary Ellen Marcy, but the engagement was called off. Marcy went on to marry George McClellan, Hill's classmate and friend from their West Point days. (loc)

A modern view of the Otto farmhouse, where John Otto, his wife, Katherine, and their four children lived at the time of the battle. The house was built in the 1830s. The Ottos had two slaves: Nancy and her son, Hillary Watson. On September 15, Confederates came to the property seeking rations upon their arrival in Sharpsburg. (cb)

covering the field south of the Boonsboro Pike, Lee knew the Federals drastically outnumbered him.

At around 2:30 p.m., Hill rode up to Lee, reporting that his men were just then crossing over the Potomac River. Lee responded with great relief, telling him, "General Hill, I was never so glad to see you." Lee ordered Hill to send his first three brigades to D. R. Jones's assistance and to keep the other two on the far-right flank to protect against any additional Federal advances from the south. While Lee knew that Hill's division would soon be there, he could only hope that Hill's advance would be quicker than that of the Federal IX Corps.

Less than 30 minutes after Hill arrived in Sharpsburg, with his men still on their way to the field, Brig. Gen. Jacob Cox gave the order that began the IX Corps assault against the Confederate right flank. Some 8,000 Federal soldiers from three divisions, spread out over the space of a mile, were aimed at the lone division of D. R. Jones. The right of the Federal advance was led by Orlando Willcox's division, with the brigades of Col. Benjamin Christ and Col. Thomas Welsh. Christ's right came near the flank of Sykes's V Corps regulars, with men from Maj. Charles Lovell's brigade advancing with their IX Corps counterparts along the southern side of the Boonsboro Pike. Behind Willcox, Col. George Crook's brigade was aligned along the creek for support. To Willcox's left was Isaac Rodman's

Col. George Crook commanded a brigade in the Kanawha Division at Antietam. Later in the war, he became a major general and saw significant action in the Shenandoah Valley in 1864. (loc)

The Sherrick farm as seen from the neighboring Otto farm in September 1862 (left). The main farmhouse was built in the late 1830s. Though Joseph Sherrick, Jr., and his wife, Sarah, owned the property, it was leased out to Leonard Emmert and his family at the time of the battle. The farm is still visible from Rodman Avenue on the way to Burnside Bridge (right). (loc)(cm)

division, with the brigades of Col. Harrison Fairchild and Col. Edward Harland—and with Col. Hugh Ewing's brigade behind in support. These IX Corps units had three batteries of artillery as well, those of Capt. George Durrell, Capt. Joseph Clark, and Lt. Charles Muhlenburg.

The Confederate line facing this massive assault consisted of the brigades of Nathan Evans, Richard Garnett, Joseph Walker, Thomas Drayton, James Kemper, and Robert Toombs, whose men were on the far right. While outnumbered by the advancing IX Corps, Jones's Confederates were supported by an impressive array of nine artillery batteries totaling over 40 guns. The Confederates also had the advantage of terrain on their side. For the Federals to reach Sharpsburg, they would have to ascend several steep ridges and a dramatic rise in the ground on their advance, all while taking infantry and artillery fire.

Shortly after 3:00 p.m., Willcox's division began its attack toward Sharpsburg. Because Willcox's men had more terrain to cover in order to strike Lee's defenses around Sharpsburg, they stepped off before Rodman's division on their left. Rodman's goal was to get to the Harpers Ferry Road, threatening Lee's flank and his possible escape route to the Potomac.

As Benjamin Christ's and Thomas Welsh's brigades traversed up the slopes toward Sharpsburg, they encountered resistance from the Virginians of Richard Garnett's brigade and the South Carolinians under Joseph Walker's command. While Christ's men were hit by enemy fire, slowing their advance, Welsh's brigade lagged on their flank, owing to the troubling terrain and the pesky Confederate skirmishers positioned in and around the Otto farm buildings.

Welsh's men were just south of the Lower Bridge Road, which ran from the Lower Bridge into Sharpsburg from the south. Walker's South Carolinians took up position along this road, some in and around a stone house and mill, further complicating Willcox's advance on Sharpsburg. As Welsh's men advanced, Lt. John Coffin came forward, bringing up two of his guns into the Otto farm orchard, attempting to provide some artillery support for the Federal attack.

Brig. Gen. Orlando Willcox's men formed the right flank of the IX Corps assault on Sharpsburg at Antietam. He is pictured here (seated) with his staff later in 1862. (loc)

To the south, Isaac Rodman soon began his own advance with Harrison Fairchild's brigade on the right and Edward Harland's on the left, pressing the brigades of James Kemper and Thomas Drayton. In the 17th Virginia of Kemper's command, the men were ordered to hold their fire until the Federal line had closed in on them. Private Alexander Hunter recalled:

As we lay there with our eyes ranging along the musket barrels, our fingers on the triggers, we saw the gilt eagles of the flagpoles emerge above the top of the hill, followed by the flags drooping on the staffs, then the tops of the blue caps appeared, and next a line of the fiercest eyes man ever looked upon. . . . Less brave, less seasoned troops would have faltered before the array of deadly tubes leveled at them, and at the recumbent line, silent, motionless and terrible, but if there was any giving away we did not see it. They fired at us before we pulled trigger and came on with vibrant shouts. Not until they were

Brig. Gen. George Sykes commanded a division in the V Corps, part of which formed alongside Willcox's right flank. Sykes's men were the only support the IX Corps had in its final assault that day. (loc)

This Edwin Forbes sketch
shows Federal soldiers
making the final push toward
Sharpsburg. (loc)

*well up in view did Colonel Corse break the silence, and
his voice was a shriek as he ordered: "FIRE!!"*

As the battle lines blazed away at each other,
men were knocked out of the ranks by the dozens.
After a lull during the early afternoon hours,
Antietam had once again reached its fever pitch,
only this time on the fields south of Sharpsburg.

Caught in the midst of the fight was Pvt. David
Thompson, one of the colorful Zouaves of the 9th
New York. Thompson recalled that "the air was full
of the hiss of bullets and the hurtle of grape shot. The
mental strain was so great that I saw at that moment
. . . the whole landscape for an instant turned slightly
red." Thompson acknowledged that in the heat of
battle, "when bullets are cracking skulls like eggshells,
the consuming passion in the breast of the average man
is to get out of the way." Thompson and his fellow New
Yorkers were raked by Southern grape shot and musket
fire, tearing apart their ranks in their push toward
Sharpsburg. In the course of its attack, Fairchild's
command lost nearly half its strength, losing 455 of its
860 men as casualties. That was the highest percentage
loss for any Federal brigade that day.

While the Confederates put up a spirited
defense, their fire could not hold the Federals for
long. Soon enough, Jones's line began to give way,
and the Confederate flank was in grave danger.
Sharpsburg became a confused and chaotic scene,
full of wounded and retreating soldiers. Robert E.
Lee now faced the very real possibility that, after
staving off defeat all day long, his luck had finally
run out. It was just past 4:00 p.m., and Union troops
were now closing in on Sharpsburg.

The Confederate commander was in the town, trying to do what he could to reinforce and restore order to the Confederate right flank in the wake of Jones's collapse. Almost as if scripted from the outset, however, it was at this moment that the first of Hill's men reached the battlefield in dramatic fashion, arriving in the right place and at the right time for the salvation of the Army of Northern Virginia.

As Hill's men entered the fight, they did not mass to go in all at once. Hill sent the brigades forward as they arrived, keeping the elements of time and surprise on their side. Brigadier General Maxcy Gregg's brigade was first, followed by the commands of Brig. Gen. James Archer and Brig. Gen. Lawrence O'Bryan Branch. Colonel John Brockenbrough and Brig. Gen. Dorsey Pender were kept in reserve with their troops, guarding the flank against any further Federal attacks.

At this crucial moment in the battle, the flank of the Federal line was in grave danger. On the far left, in Col. Edward Harland's brigade, the 16th Connecticut was marching to its infamous fate. The 16th was one of many new regiments in the Army of the Potomac that day, having been raised just weeks before in the summer of 1862. The men had received little training; according to their regimental historian, they had fired their muskets for the first time the night before the battle. Their experience at Antietam was jarring in many ways, and they were ill prepared for what they were about to face.

As Harland's brigade advanced, the veteran 8th Connecticut was on the right flank, and the 4th Rhode Island, another veteran group, was on the left flank, leaving the rookies of the 16th Connecticut in the center. During the fight, the 8th pushed far ahead of the rest of the brigade, encountering the remnants of Robert Toombs's Georgia brigade near the Harpers Ferry Road, taking heavy casualties in the process.

Toombs's men were assisted by the first elements of A. P. Hill's division to reach the field, including Captain D. G. McIntosh's artillery, which poured

Maj. Gen. Fitz John Porter, commander of the V Corps, was a close friend of George McClellan. Porter began the campaign facing charges for his conduct at Second Manassas. While McClellan was able to restore Porter's command during the Maryland campaign, he was later removed, court martialed, and cashiered from the army, though the court martial decision was overturned after the war. (loc)

Col. Joseph Walker, in the absence of Brig. Gen. Micah Jenkins, led Jenkins's brigade in combat at Antietam. (loc)

As the 9th New York pushed toward Sharpsburg, Pvt. David Thompson recalled, "the whole landscape for an instant turned slightly red." (cb)

The monument for the 9th New York Infantry is known as the "Hawkin's Zouaves." This regiment—part of Col. Harrison Fairchild's brigade—lost 235 of its 373 men, a casualty rate of 63 percent.(cb)

rounds of canister into the advancing Federals. During the attack, the 8th Connecticut lost over half its strength that day. Several IX Corps officers noted the arrival of Hill's men—Brig. Gen. Isaac Rodman among them. No sooner had Rodman sent word to Harland's left flank of this new threat than he was hit in the chest, falling to the ground with a mortal wound, and becoming the fifth general to be killed or mortally wounded that day. Just after Rodman was struck, Colonel Harland's horse was shot, causing him to rush toward his imperiled left flank on foot.

With the 8th Connecticut far ahead of the rest of the brigade, a perilous gap had opened, one which invited attack by Hill's arriving Confederates. At this crucial moment, the 16th Connecticut and 4th Rhode Island had entered a 40-acre cornfield owned by John Otto. Planted on steeply slanted ground, Otto's cornfield was difficult enough terrain to traverse without the sudden surprise that fell onto the Federals. Maxcy Gregg's South Carolinians blasted the New Englanders, sending waves of musket fire that felled men and cornstalks alike.

While the Rhode Islanders did what they could to stop Gregg's brigade, their Connecticut counterparts broke as confusion reigned supreme. Colonel Harland attempted to restore order to the scene, but the flank of his line and, in turn, the flank of the entire IX Corps's advance had dissolved in the face of Gregg's men. Jacob Bauer of the 16th Connecticut wrote home several days later, telling his wife that the Confederates "let fly a most terrific fire, we answered feebly for

This mortuary cannon marks where Brig. Gen. Isaac Rodman was mortally wounded. (cb)

about 15 minutes, when we were ordered to retreat, which was accomplished in a Bull Run fashion."

As the Connecticut men fell back, Pvt. Lester Taylor and several others came across Capt. Newton Manross, who was lying mortally wounded in the corner of Otto's cornfield. The captain had been struck by an artillery shell, and as Taylor noted, "I could look down inside of him and see his heart beat, his left shoulder all shot off." While several soldiers tried to help Manross to the rear, it was of little help. The former university professor died shortly thereafter. Private Jasper Bidwell of the 16th recalled Manross's final words, exclaiming, "My poor wife!"

With the collapse of Harland's flank, the Federal line was in trouble. Colonel Hugh Ewing brought his Ohio brigade forward to support the cratering Federal line, but now the full weight of Hill's attack was coming to bear against the Federals. On Gregg's left, the brigades of Archer and Branch were thrown into the fight, alongside the remaining portions of D. R. Jones's division.

Having come so close to the town of Sharpsburg, the men of the IX Corps now saw their attack grind to a sudden halt. Forty Confederate cannons blasted away at the Union position, while Federal gunners struggled to respond with covering fire. The brigades of Fairchild, Welsh, and Christ withdrew back toward the hills overlooking the Lower Bridge as Burnside and Cox worked to reestablish a defensive position in the wake of the sudden and dramatic Confederate counterattack. As the Confederates continued to drive the Federals back, Brig. Gen. Lawrence O'Bryan

Brig. Gen. Isaac P. Rodman, a native of Rhode Island, was a state representative and senator before the Civil War. He became the commander of the 4th Rhode Island in October 1861 and rose to become a general in the spring of 1862. After receiving a mortal wound to the chest at Antietam, Rodman died on September 30, 1862. (loc)

Lawrence O'Bryan Branch was a Democratic congressman from North Carolina before the Civil War. He commanded a brigade of soldiers in Hill's division and was killed when his brigade was pushed forward into the fighting late in the afternoon of the 17th. (loc)

A mortuary cannon for Brig. Gen. Lawrence O'Bryan Branch marks the spot of the final general officer killed during the battle. (cb)

Branch was conferring with several other commanders when he was killed instantly with a bullet to the head, becoming the third Confederate general—the sixth and final overall—to be killed or mortally wounded that day.

With a defensive position established on the heights near the Lower Bridge, the IX Corps was done for the day—as was the Union army. McClellan had placed great expectations on Burnside's late attack, hoping it could break through the Confederate lines once and for all. After Hill's counterattack, however, McClellan's mindset changed. Despite several urgent pleas to McClellan for more reserves, Burnside received no support aside from several regiments of U.S. Regulars posted on his right flank. McClellan decided against sending his available reserves—which consisted of the divisions of George Sykes and George Morrell, around 8,000 men, as well as Alfred Pleasonton's cavalry—believing they would make little difference in light of the strong Confederate counterattack.

Allegedly this decision may have been influenced by Fitz John Porter, who informed the general that his men were the last reserves of the army, and thus could not be spared. While later generations of historians would excoriate McClellan for this decision, Porter's statement was correct. His men were the army's last reserves, and given the many unknowns of the Confederate position and strength, it was reasonable to hold them back at that time.

And thus, the last attack of the Federals at Antietam had been thwarted by the timely arrival of A. P. Hill. As the sun sank slowly into the western sky, the guns of each side began to cool. A day of unparalleled slaughter in American history had at last come to a merciful end.

At the Final Attack Stop

From this tour stop, the daunting terrain south of Sharpsburg can be seen. This terrain is the most difficult that any troops encountered on the Antietam battlefield. It is best explored on the Final Attack Trail, which begins from the Burnside Bridge parking area, though it is also accessible from Branch Avenue near the monument to the 48th Pennsylvania. This is 0.2 miles south of the parking area. Look for the brown trail signs along Branch Avenue.

Branch Avenue features a cluster of several Federal monuments. (cb)

There are numerous monuments along Branch Avenue, including the mortuary cannon for Lawrence O'Bryan Branch, which is 0.3 miles south of the parking area. Branch was a three-term Democratic Congressman from North Carolina before the Civil War, and was killed at the age of 41. Isaac Rodman, the Federal division commander who was mortally wounded in the final attack, has a mortuary cannon as well, though it is only accessible via trails that leave from Branch Avenue and from the Harpers Ferry Road.

➤ TO BOTELER'S FORD
(OPTIONAL EXCURSION)

To see Boteler's Ford, where Lee retreated across the Potomac, you will need to turn left onto Harpers Ferry Road from Branch Avenue, then take the first right onto Miller's Sawmill Road. In 1.7 miles, you will reach Canal Road. Turn right and proceed 0.7 miles. There will be a small unpaved parking area on the left. Park and follow the dirt path through the trees toward the Potomac. There is a small sign for Packhorse Ford (an alternate name) along the path near the river, but there is no signage along Canal Road. If you aren't following the optional tour, directions to the next stop are at the end of chapter ten.

GPS: N 39.4308829 W 77.7774870

Lee Retreats

CHAPTER TEN

SEPTEMBER 18-20, 1862

For George McClellan, the fighting on the 17th did not end as he had hoped. While Union forces had driven the Confederates back in several areas, both armies remained on the field that night—though each had been severely bloodied.

With the fighting dwindling as darkness settled across the landscape, it was time for McClellan to plan ahead for the next day, when he intended to resume the fight. His hope was to have William Franklin and the VI Corps launch an attack on Lee's left, one that would be supported by the impending arrival of Brig. Gen. Andrew Humphreys's V Corps division. Throughout the day on the 17th, V Corps commander Fitz John Porter had been sending messages to Humphreys, trying to discern his location and when he might arrive at the battlefield. That night, Humphreys wrote back that he was still east of Frederick (his division had only left Washington on the 14th), and that his new recruits—none of whom had ever been in battle before—were struggling to keep up with the pace. To reach the army by dawn, Humphreys would have to undertake a night march of more than 20 miles with green troops. Humphreys's dispatch did not inspire confidence, telling Porter that his men would be "fit for something" in the morning. What that something was, no one knew.

Boteler's Ford today looks much as it did in 1862. The bedrock that spans the riverbottom from Maryland to West Virginia remains visible, clearly marking the ford. When water levels are low enough, the river can still be forded there. (kp)

This wartime photograph shows Boteler's Ford, where Confederates forded the Potomac after the battle of Antietam. (loc)

On the morning of the 18th, McClellan wrote several dispatches to report on what had occurred the day before, informing his wife that his handling of the battle was being described by others as "a masterpiece of art." To General Halleck in Washington, McClellan noted that the army had suffered heavy losses, but that "the battle will probably be renewed today." McClellan's message proved overly optimistic. While he had intended on continuing the battle on the morning of the 18th, circumstances caused him to change his mind.

When McClellan's reinforcements arrived—Andrew Humphreys's division and the IV Corps division of Maj. Gen. Darius Couch—they boosted Federal strength on paper alone. In reality, the troops were exhausted after marching all night and were in no condition to make an attack that morning. Thus, McClellan decided to postpone Franklin's attack. There would be no assault on the 18th. Instead, his army would rest, reorganize, and prepare for battle on the 19th.

For George McClellan, there were far too many unknowns to risk everything he had accomplished in the campaign thus far. He had successfully stopped the Confederate advance by defeating Lee at South Mountain and pinning him down in battle at Sharpsburg, just a few miles away from Virginia. At the very least, he had likely forced Lee to retreat into the Confederacy, ending the dangerous excursion into Maryland. While McClellan had not destroyed Lee's army, thus far in the campaign he had achieved the biggest success yet in the history of the Army of the Potomac.

For Robert E. Lee, the night of the 17th was one of crucial decisions as well. At his headquarters in Sharpsburg, Lee met with his leading generals to discuss the army's next move. Lee asked each officer about the status of his command and the situation along his part of the field. Many were pessimistic, telling the general that their front consisted of a thin skirmish line and not much more. Several suggested the Confederates withdraw to Virginia that night to avoid further destruction. In all likelihood, the Confederate army numbered less than 30,000 men that evening, having been bled severely throughout the day by McClellan's assaults.

While the outlook given by his leading generals was grim, Lee had other thoughts in mind. He was not yet prepared to retreat. In the three weeks since the battle of Second Manassas, Lee had come quite a distance. His army had swept through Maryland, capturing Harpers Ferry and 12,000 Federals in the process. Yet Lee still had not achieved the goal he had set at the outset of the campaign. He still wanted that elusive victory over Union forces on Union soil. Whether out of stubbornness or unfounded optimism, Lee decided to remain on the field, telling his generals, "Gentlemen, we will not cross the Potomac tonight. You will go to your respective commands, strengthen your forces. . . . If McClellan wants to fight in the morning I will give him battle again. Go!"

Lee knew that while his army had been severely battered, they had still not yet been driven from the field. If he retreated that night, however, it would guarantee a Federal victory at Antietam. Rather than hand McClellan such a grand success, Lee preferred to gamble and see what tomorrow would bring, showing once again his determination to win during the Maryland campaign.

Brig. Gen. William Pendleton was commander of the artillery reserve for the Army of Northern Virginia. He had been an Episcopal minister prior to the war. (loc)

The 18th was a day of tension as both sides waited for the battle to resume. While the Federals did receive some reinforcements, the only added strength for the Confederates came from stragglers being brought back into the lines, no doubt adding several thousand new troops to Lee's position. Each commander knew that he was taking a risk with his respective course of action; for Lee, a Federal attack could potentially destroy his army, and for McClellan, not attacking could mean allowing Lee to gather his strength and retake the initiative. However, as historian Joseph Harsh noted in his work *Taken at the Flood*, "it is difficult to conclude that either can be seriously faulted for their decisions in light of what they knew at the time and of how each interpreted his responsibility as commander of the major army of his nation. Lee believed he was compelled to take unreasonable risks. McClellan believed he was prohibited from doing so. Each may have been correct."

Ultimately, Lee was the first one to change his course. On the 18th, he expressed an interest in having Stonewall Jackson amass 50 artillery pieces and move against the Federal flank on the northern end of the field. After negative input from several officers, including artillery commander Col. Stephen D. Lee, the commanding general decided against his attack. With no further move to be made, Lee resolved to cross the Potomac River that evening and, if possible, carry on the campaign from the Virginia side. That night, as darkness fell on the battlefield, the Confederate retreat began. By 2:00 a.m., the men of Longstreet's command were splashing across the river at Boteler's Ford, and within a few hours, the rest of the Confederate army was across.

McClellan awoke on the morning of the 19th expecting his right flank to resume the fight on the northern end of the field, only to receive reports from Federal skirmishers that the Confederates had withdrawn. The Union general promptly issued orders for Brig. Gen. Alfred Pleasonton to send his cavalry forward to scout and pursue Lee's retreating

Boteler's Ford saw Union soldiers pursue Lee back into Virginia, only to be repulsed at the battle of Shepherdstown on September 19 and 20, 1862. (kp)

force, engaging the rear of the Confederate army along the river. McClellan then dispatched parts of his army to various strategic points to ensure the Confederates were retreating for good. The XII Corps was sent to Harpers Ferry to prevent Confederates from retaking the town, and the VI Corps was ordered north to Williamsport to block the Confederates from potentially crossing the river there and returning to Maryland. The V Corps was sent to Boteler's Ford to pursue the retreating enemy and add strength to Pleasonton's men.

When elements of the V Corps reached the Potomac River, they found the rear of the Confederate army. Accordingly, they acted quickly and a fight broke out, with the Federals capturing four Confederate artillery pieces. This action signaled the first day of the battle of Shepherdstown, a fight along the banks of the Potomac and the final bloodletting of the Maryland campaign. Wanting to capitalize on their success from the day before, several V Corps brigades were sent across the Potomac on the morning of September 20, hoping to strike one of Lee's retreating divisions. Rather than finding the Confederates in disarray, however, the Union soldiers encountered the division of A. P. Hill, who attacked and firmly repulsed the Union excursion on the Virginia side of the Potomac.

The battle of Shepherdstown—a Confederate victory—was a small yet consequential punctuation at the end of the Maryland campaign. While

This sketch by Alfred Waud shows Union forces at Boteler's Ford. (loc)

generations of historians have maintained that McClellan did nothing after Antietam, the Federals did indeed launch a pursuit of Lee's retreating Confederates. Moreover, by sending troops north toward Williamsport and Hagerstown, McClellan effectively ended Lee's campaign overall. Upon crossing back into Virginia, the Confederate commander had intentions of possibly crossing the river again at Williamsport, a move that would have breathed new life into the campaign. Reconnaissance by Jeb Stuart, however, proved that there was a strong presence of Union infantry and cavalry along the river there. With Federals spread out along the Maryland side of the Potomac, Lee decided to rest, remaining near Martinsburg for the time being. His attempt to seize victory in Maryland had failed.

With Lee's army back on Virginia soil, the Antietam campaign had at last come to a close. What began when D. H. Hill's division splashed across the Potomac River on September 4, 1862, ended when A. P. Hill's division repulsed the Union pursuit at Shepherdstown on September 20. In the 16 days of the campaign, the two armies had shed blood at the gaps of South Mountain, the heights around Harpers Ferry, farmers' fields around Sharpsburg, and at the Potomac near Shepherdstown. For the dead, the war was over, and the fate of the nation was unknown. For the wounded, days of agony and recovery lay ahead. For the nation, a new and uncertain future lay before it.

◢ FROM BOTELER'S FORD

If you followed the optional excursion to Boteler's Ford, continue straight ahead on Canal Road for 1.5 miles. At the intersection with state route 34, turn right and head east for 3.3 miles. You can park on the right side of the road in front of the cemetery entrance. Additional parking can be found 0.1 miles farther on your left.

GPS: N 39.46022 W 77.74182

◢ TO STOP 8

From the Final Attack parking lot, continue on Branch Avenue for 0.7 miles. At the intersection with the Harpers Ferry Road, turn right. (Note: if you would like to see the Hawkins's Zouave monument, pull over 0.3 miles ahead on the right and park on the side of the road. Use caution, as there is only room here for one or two cars at most.) To continue to the National Cemetery from Branch Avenue, proceed 0.8 miles on Harpers Ferry Road to the second stop sign, and turn right onto East Main Street. The cemetery is 0.4 miles ahead on your right. You can park on the right side of the road. Additional parking can be found 0.1 miles farther to your left.

GPS: N 39.46022 W 77.74182

America's Bloodiest Day

CHAPTER ELEVEN

When the guns fell silent at the end of the day on September 17, 1862, the suffering was only just beginning. Antietam was—and remains—the bloodiest day in American history, with more than 23,000 casualties falling in a span of 13 hours. Well over 4,000 men died in combat, and many thousands more were wounded and in dire need of medical treatment. The coming days, weeks, and months saw the death toll continue to rise as Antietam claimed more victims—some of them dying of their wounds years later.

In the hours after the fight, men of both sides were in shock at the level of violence and carnage they had witnessed. Having escaped John Otto's cornfield, Jacob Bauer of the 16th Connecticut told his wife of the "awful sight here were [sic] I am writing. The groans of the wounded the blood stained bodies [sic], and the confusion is something which no one can have any idea of unless they have been here themselves [sic]. I found war is a terrible thing even to think of but when you are actually engaged in it, it is worse yet."

Years later, in his memoir of the war, Rufus Dawes of the 6th Wisconsin noted that the sight of the battlefield at Antietam was worse than anything else he saw during his famed Civil War career: "The

"The muffle drum's sad roll has beat.
The soldier's last tattoo;
No more on life's parade shall meet.
That brave and fallen few.
On Fame's eternal camping-ground.
Their silent tents are spread,
And Glory guards, with solemn round,
The bivouac of the dead.
　　　—Theodore O'Hara
(cb)

piles of dead on the Sharpsburg and Hagerstown Pike were frightful. The 'angle of death' at Spotsylvania, and the Cold Harbor 'slaughter pen,' and the Fredericksburg Stone Wall where Sumner charged, were all mentally compared by me when I saw them, with this turnpike at Antietam. My feeling was that the Antietam turnpike surpassed all in manifest evidence of slaughter."

The carnage of which Dawes wrote lingered upon the battlefield for some time. A week after the battle, a soldier in the 107th Pennsylvania wrote home to his parents to tell them of what had happened. As part of Duryee's brigade, the 107th had opened the fight along the southern edge of the Cornfield. Upon walking across the same field, this Union private was shocked by what he saw: "On the field of battle the spot where every man fell is distinctly marked, and in places where several died the blood marks just as if a pail full had been emptied. It will take several heavy rains to wash these stains away."

In the 11th Ohio, part of George Crook's brigade in the IX Corps, Reverend William Wallace Lyle, a regimental chaplain, later recalled, "There was something inexpressibly saddening in the appearance of the Antietam battlefield. . . . It is no exaggeration to say that, on the day of dreadful conflict, the dead lay in heaps, and the

Confederate dead await burial on the southern half of the battlefield. (loc)

wounded in thousands." Upon seeing the bodies of the dead scattered about, Lyle could not help but think of their families far away:

No one, with common feelings of humanity, could look upon such terrible scenes unmoved, nor forget that around each one of the thousands of killed and wounded clustered many warm affections, and that there was no one on this bloody field so lonely, wretched, or forsaken as that for him throbbed no loving heart, and for him no tears would be shed. As I looked upon the hundreds on hundreds of killed and wounded, I thought of the distant homes of these men, and how the sunlight of hope and joy would be quenched in grief, and how mother and wife and sister would clasp their hands in speechless agony, and fathers would bow their heads and weep, as only strong men weep, when the names of loved ones were announced as among the killed or wounded or missing. Not alone on the battlefield was there agony that day! Ah! No. There was untold agony in thousands of homes far from that field of blood. Who could refrain from breathing a prayer that the Angel of the Covenant might visit every weeping household, and comfort every stricken heart? And that soon, O soon! The olive branch of peace might wave over our bleeding, distracted

Union graves line a stone wall, with Burnside Bridge in the background. (loc)

country, truth and righteousness flourish in our midst, and the people, "Walking in the light of God, In holy beauty shine."

The terrible sights spread across the field of battle. In the Sunken Road, held so valiantly by Confederates, one newspaper correspondent noted, "The Confederates had gone down as the grass falls before the scythe. . . . They were lying in rows like the ties of a railroad, in heaps, like cord-wood mingled with the splintered and shattered fence rails. Words are inadequate to portray the scene."

On the night of the 17th, the fields around Sharpsburg were filled with the screams and cries of the wounded and the lifeless forms of the dead. The dark night was punctuated by bobbing lanterns of those mercifully providing aid and taking those in need back to medical tents. At the field hospitals, surgeons worked endlessly, sawing off limbs in bloodstained aprons with little rest. One surgeon from the U.S. Sanitary Commission noted:

Indeed there is not a barn, or farmhouse, or store or church or schoolhouse, between Boonsboro and Sharpsburg, and Smoketown, that is not gorged with wounded— Rebel and Union. Even the corn-cribs, and in many instances the cow stable, and in one place the mangers were filled. Several thousands lie in open air upon straw, and all are receiving the kind services of the farmers' families and the surgeons.

Dr. Mayer, a surgeon with the 11th Connecticut, was grateful to have come through the battle alive, yet wrote, "I felt the real terror of the battle when seeing shattered limbs around me, and the terrible destruction of flesh and bone by deadly projectiles used in warfare of the present day."

The Private Soldier monument was dedicated on September 17, 1880. The soldier atop, known as "Old Simon," weighs nearly 30 tons. The monument stood at the Centennial Exposition in Philadelphia in 1876 before being taken apart and sent to Antietam. The entire monument stands 44 feet and 7 inches tall. Its inscription reads, "Not for themselves, but for their country." (cb)

Among the thousands of wounded was Sgt. Jonathan Stowe of the 15th Massachusetts, which had lost 330 casualties in the West Woods. Stowe was struck in the leg and left behind in the woods, and did not receive medical attention for two days until Union troops reached him on the 19th. He was brought into a field hospital that evening, and his leg was amputated the following day. Stowe kept record of the events surrounding his wounding and surgery in his diary, providing a stark description of his plight. He noted piles of limbs from amputations in the field hospital and his meager accommodations, including a lack of sufficient food, water, and blankets. He had trouble sleeping, noting that the nights were made long and painful, with the smell of "mortifying limbs" nearby only worsening his plight. He was treated with quinine to stave off his fever, which left him in a constant

This Gardner photograph shows the O. J. Smith farm, which was used as the field hospital for William French's II Corps division. In the aftermath of Antietam, every barn and structure in the vicinity became a field hospital of some sort. (loc)

state of thirst. As September drew to a close, Stowe hoped that the worst was behind him. He died on October 1, 1862.

For every story of wounded and dying Federal soldiers, there are similar accounts of those who wore the gray. Thomas Clark of the 5th Florida was severely wounded in the chest and leg while fighting in the Sunken Road, and after the fight, he was taken to a hospital in nearby Shepherdstown, Virginia. Clark lingered there for two months, fighting for his life while recovering from his wounds, only to die on November 11, 1862.

Clark had married Martha Law in 1858, and the couple had a young daughter, Eliza, who was born October 10, 1861. While in Shepherdstown, a local woman named Ellie Reustch cared for Clark, and upon his passing, she wrote to his widow in Florida, telling her that her husband "died in a glorious cause fighting bravely for our Independence." Clark was just one of the many soldiers who flooded the streets of towns like Shepherdstown, as the entire region was inundated with wounded men. For Mary Bedinger Mitchell, a 12-year-old resident of Shepherdstown, Antietam and its aftermath provided "an ever present sense of anguish, dread, pity, and, I fear, hatred."

As these scenes of tragedy and horror played out in hospitals all across the area, William Child,

Gardner's photograph of the David Reel farm is evidence of the cruel realities of Antietam. The barn was being used as a Confederate field hospital during the battle when it was struck by Union artillery fire, burning the wounded soldiers inside alive before they could be rescued. Bones of soldiers were later found amid the ashes of the structure. (loc)

the surgeon of the 5th New Hampshire, was among those who were forever changed by what they saw. Child described the vivid scenes around him in a letter on September 22:

> *The days after the battle are a thousand times worse than the day of the battle—and the physical pain is not the greatest pain suffered. How awful it is— you have nor can have until you see it any idea of affairs after a battle. The dead appear sickening but they suffer no pain. But the poor wounded mutilated soldiers that yet have life and sensation make a most horrid picture. I pray God may stop such infernal work—though perhaps he sent it upon us for our sins. Great indeed must have been our sins if such is our punishment.*

While the wounded suffered in the aftermath of battle, the difficult task of burying the dead began. Burial crews of soldiers were formed, and once the Confederates had left the field, bodies were found, identified if possible, and interred in the Maryland soil. One soldier in the 137th Pennsylvania described the task of burying the dead as "the most disagreeable duty that could have been assigned to us; tongue cannot describe the horrible sight." The dead were buried largely where they fell on the field, dotting the landscape with graves of individuals and burial trenches alike. Frederick Hitchcock of the 132nd Pennsylvania later noted that the work was "rough and heartless but only comporting with the character of war."

Surgeons such as Dr. Anson Hurd of the 14th Indiana worked long hours for days on end to treat thousands of wounded soldiers who flooded field hospitals across the area. (loc)

In the midst of this burial work, photographers traversed the battlefield, capturing the first-ever images of a battlefield in its true aftermath, before the dead were buried. Alexander Gardner and his assistant James Gibson spent several days, starting on the 19th, taking photographic evidence of Antietam's terrible toll. These images have lasted as some of the most visceral and stark reminders of the true cost of the American Civil War. In October 1862, they were put on display in Mathew Brady's studio in New York City, where crowds lined up around the block to see the battlefield of Antietam. In a review of the exhibit, the *New York Times* stated plainly, "Mr. Brady has done something to bring home to us the terrible reality and earnestness of war. If he has not brought bodies and laid them in our dooryards and along the streets, he has done something very like it."

At the Antietam National Cemetery

The Antietam National Cemetery is the final resting place for 4,776 Union soldiers who died during the American Civil War, as well as several hundred more post-Civil War graves of those who died or served in the Spanish American War, World War I, World War II, and the Korean War. It was created to be a burial ground for those who died

The entrance sign for Antietam National Cemetery, with the lodge building behind that once served as the park visitor center. (cb)

at the battles of South Mountain and Antietam, as well as the July 1864 battle of Monocacy in Frederick. Legislation was passed by the state of Maryland authorizing the cemetery in 1864, and it took three years to reinter the dead.

When exploring the National Cemetery, there are many notable grave sites. The most recent is that of Patrick Roy—a native of Keedysville, Maryland—who was a sailor killed in the terrorist attack on the USS *Cole* on October 12, 2000. His grave can be found near the western wall of the cemetery among other post-Civil War graves. In the back southwestern corner of the cemetery, there are several graves set apart from the rest. These are of African American World War I veterans, who were buried in a segregated section. These graves and their location show that, despite Antietam's connection to the Emancipation Proclamation, the fight for freedom and equality in the United States continues far past September 1862.

For more on Antietam National Cemetery, see Appendix B on the history of Antietam National Battlefield.

One of the great tragedies of Antietam National Cemetery is that, despite the battle there leading to the issuance of the Emancipation Proclamation, African American veterans of World War I were not buried alongside white veterans of that war. Instead, they were interred in a separate plot near the back wall of the cemetery. (cb)

A native of Washington County, Maryland, Sgt. Max Swain was killed in the opening days of the battle of the Bulge in December 1944. He was buried in an unmarked grave for several years before his remains were discovered and brought back to the United States. He was buried at Antietam National Cemetery in 1949, being one of several hundred post-Civil War soldiers to be buried at Antietam. (cb)

Antietam's most recent burial is that of Keedysville, Maryland, native Patrick Roy, a sailor on the USS *Cole* who was killed in a terrorist attack on October 12, 2000. Fireman Roy was 19 years old when he died. He had grown up visiting Antietam National Battlefield, even helping to clean headstones in the cemetery. Although the cemetery had been closed to new burials for nearly 50 years, an exception was made for Roy. (cb)

The grave of Capt. Werner von Bachelle, 2nd Wisconsin. Bachelle was an immigrant to the United States, having previously served in the French army. As Maj. Rufus Dawes wrote of him in his memoirs, "His soldierly qualities commanded the respect of all, and his loss was deeply felt in the regiment." Bachelle also had a Newfoundland dog with him. When he was killed, the dog was with him—and remained with his body as the battle continued. Two days later, on September 19, the dog was found dead, still lying with Bachelle. The two were buried together on the field, and were likely reinterred together in Antietam National Cemetery. (cb)

This is the grave of Color Sgt. George Simpson, Company C, 125th Pennsylvania, killed behind the Dunker Church in the West Woods. (cb)

Headstone for Lt. John Lantry, 8th Ohio, who was killed by an artillery shell while attacking Confederates at the Sunken Road. Lantry's mother, Mary, applied for a mother's pension after John's death because her 70-year-old husband, James, was unable to work and the couple had relied upon their son for financial support. While Mary received her pension, nothing could replace her son. (cb)

Thenceforward and Forever Free

President Abraham Lincoln altered the course of the Civil War and the nation when he issued the preliminary Emancipation Proclamation five days after the battle. During the summer of 1862, he agonized over issuing a proclamation to abolish slavery in those states in rebellion. Some of his cabinet thought that such a move would look like an act of desperation in the face of Union military setbacks. The president needed a victory to give him the opportunity for such a move. The Battle of Antietam, followed by Lee's withdrawal to Virginia, was the decisive moment.

The proclamation was issued in two parts. The preliminary document was introduced on September 22, 1862 and the final on January 1, 1863. Both documents freed slaves in those states in rebellion. In addition to setting the stage for the abolition of slavery in 1865, it was a decisive war measure. The proclamation went far in discouraging European nations from allying with the Confederacy. It also deprived the South of valuable labor for their war effort and led to the recruitment of almost 200,000 African American soldiers for the Union cause.

MEN OF COLOR. TO ARMS! NOW OR NEVER!

Thenceforward and Forever Free

EPILOGUE

SEPTEMBER 22, 1862

More than 150 years later, Antietam still stands as a landmark day in the history of the country. In October 1862, Pvt. Frank Bullard of the 15th Massachusetts attempted to convey what Antietam meant in a letter home to his aunt, telling her that it had been "the most desperate battle of the war, where thousands yielded their lives that this government must and shall live."

Bullard's words provide a fitting description of the importance of Antietam; it was a battle marked by desperation on both sides, as the future of the country was very much at stake. Had Lee and the Confederates been successful, then an unchecked and victorious Southern army on northern soil could have spelled doom for the Union in the autumn of 1862. England and France were each on the verge of recognizing the Confederacy, Confederate forces were advancing into Kentucky in the West, and the Lincoln administration was having an increasingly difficult time maintaining the North's will for victory. Certainly, a Confederate victory at Antietam could have changed the course of history, possibly leading to European recognition of the South coupled with deep political and military setbacks for the

A display in the battlefield visitor center highlights the important impact of the Emancipation Proclamation, forever tied to events on the field at Antietam. (cm)

In early October, President Lincoln visited the Army of the Potomac, which was still camped near Sharpsburg. He was photographed with McClellan and the commanders of the army. (loc)

North. Lee's retreat back into Virginia following Antietam signaled the end of a grand Confederate opportunity in September 1862. While Lee and his army would come perilously close to victory again in July 1863 at Gettysburg, Antietam very well may have been the Confederacy's High Water Mark.

It is for all these reasons that Antietam was a Union victory. Despite conventional wisdom long hailing the battle as a stalemate, Union forces were successful in stopping the Confederate tide in Maryland. George McClellan was able to quickly and efficiently rebuild an entire army in the span of just a few days in early September 1862. He then advanced through Maryland, fought two major battles, and forced Confederates to retreat back into Virginia. All this was done in the span of just over two weeks. Certainly, Antietam had its share of missed opportunities, as any battle does. However, we must not allow missed opportunities to distract from the larger picture.

Throughout the day on September 17, Federal forces repeatedly drove back Confederate troops, and if not for several well-timed and well-placed counterattacks by Lee, the war very possibly could have ended that day. Just because it did not does not lessen Antietam's meaning. Antietam was not a tactical stalemate. Through multiple assaults and ferocious fighting, the Army of the Potomac

Lincoln and McClellan met at the general's headquarters. The two men did not share a common view of the war and its objectives, and Lincoln's Emancipation Proclamation only widened the gap between them. After McClellan was relieved of command in November 1862, he went on to become the Democratic nominee for president in 1864, running against—and losing to—Lincoln that fall. (loc)

damaged the Army of Northern Virginia so severely that, despite waiting a day, Lee was forced to retreat from the field. It was a victory for the Union and a defeat for the Confederacy.

And yet, perhaps the most powerful aspect of Antietam's legacy is its connection with the future of freedom in the United States. When the campaign began, President Lincoln was on the verge of issuing a history-altering directive, declaring that all slaves in the southern states in rebellion would be free under his authority as commander in chief. Lincoln had resolved to issue this proclamation of emancipation the previous July, but wanting the measure to have the strength of a Union victory, he had postponed it until one could be delivered. When the Maryland campaign

The Federal loss at Fredericksburg in December threatened to undercut the Emancipation Proclamation because Lincoln could not demonstrate an ability to enforce his lofty goals. (nps)

Francis Carpenter's *First Reading of the Emancipation Proclamation*, an 1864 painting, depicts Lincoln and his cabinet discussing the Emancipation Proclamation. Antietam's link to the Emancipation Proclamation may be the most significant result of the battle. The final Emancipation Proclamation, issued January 1, 1863, was, in Lincoln's own words, "the central act of my administration, and the great event of the nineteenth century." (loc)

began, Lincoln later recalled, he made a solemn promise to himself and to God that should the Confederates be driven from Union soil, he would have the victory for which he had been waiting and he would issue his proclamation.

During the campaign, Lincoln anxiously awaited word from the front. In the aftermath of Antietam, he waited still, hoping to hear that Lee's army had been defeated and driven out of Maryland. Once he knew for certain that Lee's campaign had come to a close, Lincoln resolved to seize the moment. He spent Sunday, September 21 in his office, working and revising the text of his original proclamation draft, preparing it for the eyes of the nation, and indeed the world. The following day, Lincoln held a cabinet meeting at the Executive Mansion, where he informed his cabinet of his solemn oath to God above that he would issue the proclamation if Lee's army was pushed out of Maryland. "The rebel army is now driven out, and I am going to fulfill that promise," the president declared. He then proceeded to read the four pages which he had prepared the day before. The preliminary Emancipation Proclamation declared that, as of January 1, 1863, all slaves in those states then in rebellion against the federal government would be "then, thenceforward, and forever free."

The reaction to the proclamation was mixed, though its impact was profound. England and France, which had flirted with the idea of recognizing the Confederacy as a separate and independent nation, now recoiled from doing so. Not only had Lee's setback at Antietam dissuaded

Sculpted by Ed Hamilton and completed in 1997, the *Spirit of Freedom* stands at the center of the African American Civil War Memorial in Washington, D.C., at the corner of Vermont Avenue, 10th Street, and U Street NW. The memorial lists the names of more than 220,000 men—mostly of African descent—who served with the United States Colored Troops and in the U.S. Navy during the war. (nps)

them, but they were loath to recognize a nation fighting on the side of slavery in the wake of the proclamation. In the South, the proclamation was greeted with scorn and derision. When the final version was issued, Confederate President Jefferson

Davis called it "the most execrable measure in the history of guilty man."

Even in the Union ranks, many soldiers voiced disagreement, believing they were fighting a war for the Union alone, not one of abolition. In time, many would come to embrace the proclamation, but one who remained in opposition to it was George McClellan, who thought it would only further rile up the South and do little to help bring the war to a close.

As it was, McClellan was a man not long for his post. Several weeks after Antietam, Lincoln visited the Army of the Potomac, which was still based around Sharpsburg. Lincoln's visit was fraught with tension between the president and his general. While Lincoln encouraged McClellan to begin a new campaign, in the weeks that followed, McClellan stayed put and attempted to rebuild the Army of the Potomac as he saw fit. McClellan envisioned another grand campaign toward Richmond, one that required lots of preparation. While McClellan had his reasons for his delays, they ultimately proved too much for Lincoln. Even once the army was on the move, the president's frustrations boiled over, and McClellan was relieved of his command on November 7, 1862. His war had come to an end.

The following month, McClellan's replacement, Ambrose Burnside, led the army to a disastrous defeat against Lee at Fredericksburg, Virginia, and the bloodshed continued. Indeed, when Lincoln issued the final Emancipation Proclamation on January 1, 1863, the war was not yet halfway over. The promise of freedom enshrined in that proclamation was still far from being won. The killing would continue, growing exponentially costlier for the nation for each year of combat. Chancellorsville, Gettysburg, Chickamauga, the Wilderness, Spotsylvania, Cold Harbor, Petersburg, the Atlanta campaign, and so many others still lay ahead. Many of those who had escaped the slaughter of Antietam would fall on other battlefields across the nation.

As the war progressed, however, it became a fundamentally different type of war. It was changed forever by the events of one day: September 17, 1862. Before Antietam, it was a war for the restoration of the Union as it once was, one with slavery intact. After Antietam, the war was one being waged for a new and better Union, one without slavery. The Emancipation Proclamation had forever changed the future of the country. As newspaperman Horace Greeley proclaimed in the *New York Tribune*, "It is the beginning of the end of the rebellion; the beginning of the new life of the nation."

For both the North and the South, the stakes had been raised, and the price of defeat was made clear. Antietam was not only the costliest day of the war, and not only had it stymied Lee's invasion of Maryland, but in its impact on Lincoln and the Emancipation Proclamation, it may very well have been the most consequential day of the war. Rarely has the link between bloodshed on the battlefield and the freedom of millions been so clear and so direct as it was on the farm fields of western Maryland in September 1862.

Presidential Visits to Antietam

APPENDIX A

Ever since the battle was fought, Antietam has seen countless visitors make the pilgrimage to its fields, attempting to understand and commemorate what took place there. This includes eight different sitting presidents, each of whom came to Antietam either to pay their respects or to speak on the meaning of the battle— and each, in turn, shaping how the nation looked back on its bloodiest day.

The first president to visit Antietam was Abraham Lincoln, who traveled to Sharpsburg, Maryland, in early October 1862, just a few weeks after the battle. Lincoln wanted to confer with Maj. Gen. George B. McClellan and ascertain what might come next for the recently victorious Army of the Potomac. Though Lincoln urged McClellan to begin a new campaign against Lee's Confederates, McClellan was reluctant to do so until he felt his army was ready. Ultimately, Lincoln removed McClellan from command one month later, a decision no doubt influenced by the president's visit to the battlefield.

Several years after Lincoln's visit— and under vastly different circumstances— his successor, Andrew Johnson, made his own trip to Sharpsburg, this time for the dedication of the Antietam National Cemetery on September 17, 1867, honoring the nearly 5,000 Union dead buried there. Johnson's speech lacked the eloquent prose and soaring themes of Lincoln's Gettysburg Address, saying nothing about the reasons why the war was fought. Instead, Johnson simply called the nation to focus on peace and reconciliation. Many Republicans were highly critical of his remarks— just as they were of Johnson's lenient Reconstruction policies toward the South.

William McKinley came to Antietam as a soldier, returned as president, and was memorialized there after his death. (cm)

Antietam's next presidential visit occurred on October 14, 1869, when Ulysses S. Grant returned to see the battlefield (he had attended the dedication of the cemetery in 1867 in his role as general-in-chief). Grant's visit was rather informal, and he was accompanied that day by William T. Sherman, his friend and former Civil War general.

It was not until the dawn of the twentieth Century that a president would again come to Antietam. When he had last been there, William McKinley served as a 19-year-old commissary sergeant in the 23rd Ohio in 1862; on May 30, 1900, when he returned to speak at the dedication of the Maryland Monument, he was the 25th President of the United States. In McKinley's speech, he too called for reconciliation, referring to both sides as Americans: "The valor of the one or the other, the valor of both, is the common heritage of us all. . . ." Of course, McKinley's speech did not mention the failures of Reconstruction or abuses of civil rights for African Americans. Those themes were not prevalent in how the war was remembered in 1900, even for many Union veterans of the battle.

A photo from a park display shows historian Robert Lagemann and President John F. Kennedy at Burnside Bridge in 1963. "Antietam symbolizes something even more important than combat heroism and military strategy," JFK said. "It marks a diplomatic turning point of world-wide consequence. From this point onward, our Civil War had a new dimension which was important to the whole course of human liberty." (nps)

Three years later, McKinley's successor, President Theodore Roosevelt, visited Antietam on September 17, 1903, to speak at the dedication of the New Jersey State Monument. Born during the war, Roosevelt was the youngest man to have ever become president when he assumed the office after McKinley's assassination. His speech thanked the veterans present, noting, "It was because you, the men who wear the button of the Grand Army, triumphed in those dark years, that every American now holds his head high, proud in the knowledge that he belongs to a nation whose glorious past and great present will be succeeded by an even mightier future." He noted that the Union victory in the Civil War was for the welfare of all mankind, and it was incumbent on the leaders of the day to carry on the work that the Union army had accomplished 41 years before.

Several decades passed before Antietam again saw a sitting president. This time, it was Franklin Delano Roosevelt who, on September 17, 1937, took part in the commemoration of the battle's 75th anniversary. With the nation in the midst of the Great Depression, Roosevelt carried on the theme from other presidential addresses at Antietam, focusing on reconciliation. It did no good "to discuss again the rights and wrongs" of the war, Roosevelt noted, but that it was best for the American people to unite together as one. Roosevelt called for a national focus to meet challenges facing the country, referring to the "unity of understanding which is so increasingly ours today." Yet again, a sitting president used conflict in the past to call for a more united present.

When Teddy Roosevelt came to Antietam in 1903 for the dedication of the New Jersey Monument, he represented a new generation of leadership. (nps)

Franklin Roosevelt was the last president to deliver an address at Antietam. Only two presidents since—John F. Kennedy in 1963 and Jimmy Carter in 1978—have come to the battlefield. For those who did come to Antietam to speak on the battle's meaning, however, their remarks showed a clear focus on reunion, reconciliation, and moving forward as one country. There was little interest in reminding the country of why the war was fought or of the failures of Reconstruction, which certainly shows the larger problems the United States has faced in remembering the war and its impact on all Americans. Instead, these presidents used Antietam and the war to remind the country to stay united in the present and future, hoping America would never again see such a day as September 17, 1862.

A History of Antietam National Battlefield

APPENDIX B

BY BRIAN BARACZ

The first step in remembering the tragic day that was Antietam came rather quickly following the battle. Burying the dead and the creation of the National Cemetery preceded any attempt to preserve any part of the battlefield.

Following Lee's retreat back into Virginia, Federal forces buried their own and then the Confederate dead. It is difficult to arrive upon an exact number, but approximately 7,000 died on the day of and the days following the fight. They were interred throughout the fields that surrounded the Sharpsburg area.

In his claim to the government for damages incurred during the battle, William Roulette said he had 700 soldiers buried on his property. Another farmer claimed that as he plowed his fields, he just pulled up the headboards and continued on with his work. The citizens of Sharpsburg needed assistance if they were to survive in the area.

The first assistance came from the State of Maryland, which passed legislation in 1864 to create a cemetery for those killed at Antietam. Ground was purchased the next year, and funding was provided by Northern states. By 1867, the cemetery was complete, and a formal dedication was held that year on September 17, the fifth anniversary of the battle. It was widely attended by veterans and President Andrew Johnson provided remarks.

Though initial plans for the Antietam Cemetery called for both Union and Confederate soldiers to be buried there, no Confederates were knowingly included in the cemetery. Confederate soldiers remained

Constructed by the War Department in 1897 as part of its efforts to use the Antietam battlefield as an outdoor classroom, the observation tower at the end of the Sunken Road stands nearly 60 feet tall. It offers a 360-degree view of the battlefield, much of which still remained in private hands when the tower was constructed. (cm)

The observation tower, when originally constructed, had no roof. (nps)

One of the earliest historians of the battle was Ezra Carman, who'd fought at Antietam as a colonel in the 13th New Jersey. The Antietam Battlefield Board hired him in the early twentieth century to write text for interpretive signs and assist with the creation of a series of troop movement maps. His account of the battle was issued in an updated, three-volume edition edited by historian Tom Clemens in 2010-16. (nps)

in the fields where they were originally buried, and in some cases, remained in those battlefield graves up to seven years. At that point the State of Maryland provided the funding to remove them to one of three local, town cemeteries: Mount Olivet Cemetery in Frederick, Maryland, Rose Hill Cemetery in Hagerstown, Maryland, as well as Elmwood Cemetery in Shepherdstown, West Virginia.

As for the battlefield proper, legislation passed in 1890 was the first step in creating what we know today as Antietam National Battlefield. It was through the work of three groups, working together, that the idea originated to establish and preserve five Civil War battlefields. The veterans of the war, Congress, and the U.S. War Department deemed Chickamauga and Chattanooga, Gettysburg, Vicksburg, Shiloh, and Antietam to be set aside for future generations to visit and reflect upon the American Civil War.

In addition to being places of reflection, these original five battlefields became outdoor classrooms for the military. During a tour, or "staff ride," it is not so much the minutia of battle that is studied, but rather leadership roles and decisions that were made during the battle and campaign. Staff rides of the battlefield are still conducted today for all branches of the military.

The initial plan for the establishment of each of these initial five parks was unique. Unlike the other four battlefields, at Antietam, just enough land was acquired so that a five-mile road system could be constructed through the battleground, which equaled about 65 acres. In addition to a roadway, the battle lines were established and marked by iron tablets. A stone observation tower was constructed near the Sunken Road in 1897 which allowed visitors to get an elevated view of the field. Towers,

More than 10,000 people attended the National Cemetery dedication in 1867—including President Andrew Johnson and governors from seven states. (nps)

tablets, and tour roads are all consistent features of the War Department battlefields.

The U.S. War Department was the caretaker of these five battlefields for several decades, as well as others that were established in the early 1900s. It was during a period of reorganization of the government in 1933 that these battlefields were then transferred to the National Park Service.

At Antietam, there are a little more than 3,000 acres within the legislative boundary set up by the War Department. As of 2017, more than 2,300

acres are owned by the federal government. The real success story at Antietam is that 60 percent of those 2,300 acres has been acquired within the last 15 years.

A private souvenir stand once stood next to the Sunken Road, offering refreshments and battlefield mementos. (nps)

BRIAN BARACZ is a park ranger for the National Park Service at Antietam National Battlefield in Sharpsburg, Maryland.

"Many nations have gone into decay and oblivion by the indifference and apathy of their citizens; ours will be no exception unless our people maintain and preserve it with devoted loyalty. If the same sublime patriotism manifested by you on this battlefield and in your lives since is maintained and perpetuated by the citizens of this country, then our Republic will be forever safe and will ascend to even higher and more exalted civilization and a purer destiny."

– General Nelson Miles
Dedication of the New York Monument
September 17, 1920 (cm)

Order of Battle
BATTLE OF ANTIETAM
SEPTEMBER 17, 1862

ARMY OF THE POTOMAC
Maj. Gen. George B. McClellan

FIRST CORPS Maj. Gen. Joseph Hooker; Brig. Gen. George Meade
FIRST DIVISION Brig. Gen. Abner Doubleday
First Brigade Col. Walter Phelps, Jr.
22nd New York • 24th New York • 30th New York • 84th New York (14th Brooklyn)
2nd US Sharpshooters

Second Brigade Lt. Col. William Hoffman
7th Indiana • 76th New York • 95th New York • 56th Pennsylvania

Third Brigade Brig. Gen. Marsena Patrick
21st New York • 23rd New York • 35th New York • 80th New York

Fourth Brigade Brig. Gen. John Gibbon
19th Indiana • 2nd Wisconsin • 6th Wisconsin • 7th Wisconsin

Artillery Capt. J. Albert Monroe
New Hampshire Light, 1st Battery • 1st Rhode Island Light, Battery D
1st New York Light, Battery L • 4th United States, Battery B

SECOND DIVISION Brig. Gen. James Ricketts
First Brigade Brig. Gen. Abram Duryee
97th New York • 104th New York • 105th New York • 107th Pennsylvania

Second Brigade Col. William Christian; Col. Peter Lyle
26th New York • 94th New York • 88th Pennsylvania • 90th Pennsylvania

Third Brigade Brig. Gen. George Hartsuff; Col. Richard Coulter
16th Maine • 12th Massachusetts • 13th Massachusetts • 83rd Pennsylvania
11th Pennsylvania

Artillery
1st Pennsylvania Light, Battery F • Pennsylvania Light, Battery C

THIRD DIVISION Brig. Gen. George Meade; Brig. Gen. Truman Seymour
First Brigade Brig. Gen. Truman Seymour; Col. R. Biddle Roberts
1st Pennsylvania Reserves • 2nd Pennsylvania Reserves • 6th Pennsylvania Reserves
13th Pennsylvania Reserves

Second Brigade Col. Albert Magilton
3rd Pennsylvania Reserves • 4th Pennsylvania Reserves • 7th Pennsylvania Reserves
8th Pennsylvania Reserves

Third Brigade Lt. Col. Robert Anderson
9th Pennsylvania Reserves • 10th Pennsylvania Reserves • 11th Pennsylvania Reserves
12th Pennsylvania Reserves

Artillery
1st Pennsylvania Light, Battery A • 1st Pennsylvania Light, Battery B
5th United States, Battery C

SECOND CORPS Maj. Gen. Edwin V. Sumner
FIRST DIVISION Maj. Gen. Israel Richardson; Brig. Gen. John C. Caldwell;
Brig. Gen. Winfield Hancock
First Brigade Brig. Gen. John C. Caldwell
5th New Hampshire • 7th New York • 61st New York • 64th New York
81st Pennsylvania

Second Brigade Brig. Gen. Thomas Meagher; Col. John Burke
29th Massachusetts • 63rd New York • 69th New York • 88th New York

Third Brigade Col. John Brooke
2nd Delaware • 52nd New York • 57th New York • 66th New York
53rd Pennsylvania

Artillery
1st New York Light, Battery B • 5th United States, Batteries A and C

SECOND DIVISION Maj. Gen. John Sedgwick; Brig. Gen. Oliver O. Howard
First Brigade Brig. Gen. Willis Gorman
15th Massachusetts • 1st Minnesota • 34th New York • 82nd New York
Massachusetts Sharpshooters, 1st Company • Minnesota Sharpshooters, 2nd Company

Second Brigade Brig. Gen. Oliver O. Howard; Col. Joshua T. Owen;
Col. DeWitt C. Baxter
69th Pennsylvania • 71st Pennsylvania • 72nd Pennsylvania • 106th Pennsylvania

Third Brigade Brig. Gen. N. J. T. Dana; Col. Norman Hall
19th Massachusetts • 20th Massachusetts • 7th Michigan • 42nd New York
59th New York

Artillery
1st Rhode Island Light, Battery A • 1st United States, Battery I

THIRD DIVISION Brig. Gen. William H. French
First Brigade Brig. Gen. Nathan Kimball
14th Indiana • 8th Ohio • 132nd Pennsylvania • 7th West Virginia

Second Brigade Col. Dwight Morris
14th Connecticut • 108th New York • 130th Pennsylvania

Third Brigade Brig. Gen. Max Weber; Col. John Andrews
1st Delaware • 5th Maryland • 4th New York

Unattached Artillery
1st New York Light, Battery G • 1st Rhode Island Light, Battery B
1st Rhode Island Light, Battery G

FOURTH CORPS—FIRST DIVISION Maj. Gen. Darius Couch
First Brigade Brig. Gen. Charles Devens, Jr.
7th Massachusetts • 10th Massachusetts • 36th New York • 2nd Rhode Island

Second Brigade Brig. Gen. Albion P. Howe
62nd New York • 93rd Pennsylvania • 98th Pennsylvania • 102nd Pennsylvania
139th Pennsylvania

Third Brigade Brig. Gen. John Cochrane
65th New York • 67th New York • 122nd New York • 23rd Pennsylvania
61st Pennsylvania • 82nd Pennsylvania

Artillery
New York Light, 3rd Battery • *1st Pennsylvania Light, Battery C*
1st Pennsylvania Light, Battery D • *2nd United States, Battery G*

FIFTH CORPS Maj. Gen. Fitz John Porter
First Division Maj. Gen. George Morrell
First Brigade Col. James Barnes
2nd Maine • *18th Massachusetts* • *1st Michigan* • *13th New York*
25th New York • *118th Pennsylvania* • *Massachusetts Sharpshooters, 2nd Company*

Second Brigade Brig. Gen. Charles Griffin
2nd District of Columbia • *9th Massachusetts* • *32nd Massachusetts*
4th Michigan • *14th New York* • *62nd Pennsylvania*

Third Brigade Col. T. B. W. Stockton
20th Maine • *16th Michigan* • *12th New York* • *17th New York*
44th New York • *83rd Pennsylvania* • *Michigan Sharpshooters, Brady's Company*

Artillery
Massachusetts Light, Battery C • *1st Rhode Island Light, Battery C*
5th United States, Battery D

Second Division Brig. Gen. George Sykes
First Brigade Lt. Col. Robert Buchanan
3rd United States • *4th United States* • *12th United States, 1st and 2nd Battalions*
14th United States, 1st and 2nd Battalions

Second Brigade Maj. Charles Lovell
1st and 6th United States • *2nd and 10th United States* • *11th United States*
17th United States

Third Brigade Col. Gouverneur K. Warren
5th New York • *10th New York*

Artillery
1st United States, Batteries E and G • *5th United States, Battery I*
5th United States, Battery K

Third Division Brig. Gen. Andrew Humphreys
First Brigade Brig. Gen. Erastus B. Tyler
91st Pennsylvania • *126th Pennsylvania* • *129th Pennsylvania* • *134th Pennsylvania*

Second Brigade Col. Peter Allabach
123rd Pennsylvania • 131st Pennsylvania • 133rd Pennsylvania
155th Pennsylvania

Artillery Capt. Lucius Robinson
1st New York Light, Battery C • 1st Ohio Light, Battery L

ARTILLERY RESERVE Lt. Col. William Hays
1st Battalion New York Light, Battery A • 1st Battalion New York Light, Battery B
1st Battalion New York Light, Battery C • 1st Battalion New York Light, Battery D
New York Light, 5th Battery • 1st United States, Battery K
4th United States, Battery G

SIXTH CORPS Maj. Gen. William B. Franklin
FIRST DIVISION Maj. Gen. Henry W. Slocum
First Brigade Col. Alfred T. A. Tolbert
1st New Jersey • 2nd New Jersey • 3rd New Jersey • 4th New Jersey

Second Brigade Col. Joseph J. Bartlett
5th Maine • 16th New York • 27th New York • 96th Pennsylvania

Third Brigade Brig. Gen. John Newton
18th New York • 31st New York • 32nd New York • 95th Pennsylvania

Artillery Capt. Emory Upton
Maryland Light, Battery A • Massachusetts Light, Battery A
New Jersey Light, Battery A • 2nd United States, Battery D

SECOND DIVISION Maj. Gen. William F. Smith
First Brigade Winfield S. Hancock; Col. Amasa Cobb
6th Maine • 43rd New York • 49th Pennsylvania • 137th New York
5th Wisconsin

Second Brigade Brig. Gen. W. T. H. Brooks
2nd Vermont • 3rd Vermont • 4th Vermont • 5th Vermont • 6th Vermont

Third Brigade Col. William H. Irwin
7th Maine • 20th New York • 33rd New York • 49th New York • 77th New York

Artillery Capt. Romeyn B. Ayres
Maryland Light, Battery B • New York Light, 1st Battery • 5th United States, Battery F

NINTH CORPS Maj. Gen. Ambrose Burnside; Maj. Gen. Jesse Reno; Brig. Gen. Jacob Cox
FIRST DIVISION Brig. Gen. Orlando Willcox
First Brigade Col. Benjamin Crist
28th Massachusetts • 17th Michigan • 79th New York • 50th Pennsylvania

Second Brigade Col. Thomas Welsh
8th Michigan • 46th New York • 45th Pennsylvania • 100th Pennsylvania

Artillery
Massachusetts Light, 8th Battery • 2nd United States, Battery E

SECOND DIVISION Brig. Gen. Samuel Sturgis
First Brigade Brig. Gen. James Nagle
2nd Maryland • 6th New Hampshire • 9th New Hampshire • 48th Pennsylvania

Second Brigade Brig. Gen. Edward Ferrero
21st Massachusetts • 35th Massachusetts • 51st New York • 51st Pennsylvania

Artillery
Pennsylvania Light, Battery D • 4th United States, Battery E

THIRD DIVISION Brig. Gen. Isaac P. Rodman; Col. Edward Harland
First Brigade Col. Harrison Fairchild
9th New York • 89th New York • 103rd New York

Second Brigade Col. Edward Harland
8th Connecticut • 11th Connecticut • 16th Connecticut • 4th Rhode Island

Artillery
5th United States, Battery A

KANAWHA DIVISION Brig. Gen. Jacob Cox; Col. Eliakim Scammon
First Brigade Col. Eliakim Scammon; Col. Hugh Ewing
12th Ohio • 23rd Ohio • 30th Ohio • Ohio Light Artillery, 1st Battery
West Virginia Cavalry, Gilmore's Company • West Virginia Cavalry, Harrison's Company

Second Brigade Col. George Crook
11th Ohio • 28th Ohio • 36th Ohio • Schambeck's Company, Chicago Dragoons
Kentucky Light Artillery, Simmonds's Battery

Unattached Cavalry and Artillery
6th New York Cavalry • Ohio Cavalry, Third Independent Company
3rd United States, Batteries L and M • 2nd New York, Battery L

TWELFTH CORPS Maj. Gen. Joseph K. F. Mansfield; Brig. Gen. Alpheus
S. Williams
FIRST DIVISION Brig. Gen. Alpheus S. Williams; Brig. Gen. Samuel W. Crawford;
Brig. Gen. George H. Gordon
First Brigade Brig. Gen. Samuel W. Crawford; Col. Joseph Knipe
5th Connecticut • 10th Maine • 28th New York • 46th Pennsylvania
124th Pennsylvania • 125th Pennsylvania • 128th Pennsylvania

Third Brigade Brig. Gen. George H. Gordon; Col. Thomas H. Ruger
27th Indiana • 2nd Massachusetts (Zouaves d'Afrique attached)
13th New Jersey • 107th New York • 3rd Wisconsin

SECOND DIVISION Brig. Gen. George S. Greene
First Brigade Lt. Col. Hector Tyndale; Maj. Orrin Crane
5th Ohio • 7th Ohio • 29th Ohio • 66th Ohio • 28th Pennsylvania

Second Brigade Col. Henry J. Stainrook
3rd Maryland • 102nd New York • 109th Pennsylvania • 111th Pennsylvania

Third Brigade Col. William B. Goodrich; Lt. Col. Jonathan Austin
3rd Delaware • Purnell Legion, Maryland • 60th New York • 78th New York

ARTILLERY Capt. Clermont L. Best
Maine Light, 4th Battery • Maine Light, 6th Battery • 1st New York Light, Battery M
• New York Light, 10th Battery • Pennsylvania Light, Battery E • Pennsylvania Light,
Battery F • 4th United States, Battery F

CAVALRY DIVISION Brig. Gen. Alfred Pleasonton
First Brigade Maj. Charles Whiting
5th United States • 6th United States

Second Brigade Col. John Farnsworth
8th Illinois • 3rd Indiana • 1st Massachusetts • 8th Pennsylvania

Third Brigade Col. Richard Rush
4th Pennsylvania • 6th Pennsylvania

Fourth Brigade Col. Andrew McReynolds
1st New York • 12th Pennsylvania

Fifth Brigade Col. Benjamin Davis
8th New York • 3rd Pennsylvania

Artillery
2nd United States, Battery A • 2nd United States, Batteries B and L
2nd United States, Battery M • 3rd United States, Batteries C and G

Unattached
1st Maine Cavalry • 15th Pennsylvania Cavalry

ARMY OF NORTHERN VIRGINIA
Gen. Robert E. Lee

LONGSTREET'S COMMAND Maj. Gen. James Longstreet
McLAWS'S DIVISION Maj. Gen. Lafayette McLaws
Kershaw's Brigade Brig. Gen. Joseph B. Kershaw
2nd South Carolina • 3rd South Carolina • 7th South Carolina • 8th South Carolina

Semmes's Brigade Brig. Gen. Paul Semmes
10th Georgia • 53rd Georgia • 15th Virginia • 32nd Virginia

Cobb's Brigade Brig. Gen. Howell Cobb; Lt. Col. C. C. Sanders; Lt. Col. William MacRae
16th Georgia • 24th Georgia • Cobb's Legion (GA) • 15th North Carolina

Barksdale's Brigade Brig. Gen. William Barksdale
13th Mississippi • 17th Mississippi • 18th Mississippi • 21st Mississippi

Artillery Col. H. C. Cabell
Manley's (NC) Battery • Pulaski (GA) Artillery • Richmond (Fayette) Artillery
Richmond Howitzers, First Company • Troup (GA) Artillery

ANDERSON'S DIVISION Maj. Gen. Richard H. Anderson
Wilcox's Brigade Col. Alfred Cumming
8th Alabama • 9th Alabama • 10th Alabama • 11th Alabama

Armistead's Brigade Brig. Gen. Lewis A. Armistead; Col. J. G. Hodges
9th Virginia • 14th Virginia • 38th Virginia • 53rd Virginia • 57th Virginia

Mahone's Brigade Col. William A. Parham
6th Virginia • 12th Virginia • 16th Virginia • 41st Virginia • 61st Virginia

Pryor's Brigade Brig. Gen. Roger A. Pryor
14th Alabama • 2nd Florida • 8th Florida • 3rd Virginia • 5th Florida

Featherston's Brigade Brig. Gen. Winfield S. Featherston; Col. Carnot Posey
12th Mississippi • 16th Mississippi • 19th Mississippi • 2nd Mississippi Battalion

Wright's Brigade Brig. Gen. Ambrose R. Wright
44th Alabama • 3rd Georgia • 22nd Georgia • 48th Georgia

Artillery Maj. John S. Saunders
*Donaldsonville (LA) Artillery • Huger's (VA) Battery • Moorman's (VA) Battery
Thompson's (Grimes's, VA) Battery*

JONES'S DIVISION Brig. Gen. David R. Jones
Toombs's Brigade Brig. Gen. Robert Toombs; Col. Henry Benning
2nd Georgia • 15th Georgia • 17th Georgia • 20th Georgia

Drayton's Brigade Brig. Gen. Thomas F. Drayton
50th Georgia • 51st Georgia • 15th South Carolina • 3rd South Carolina Battalion

Garnett's Brigade Brig. Gen. R. B. Garnett
8th Virginia • 18th Virginia • 19th Virginia • 28th Virginia • 56th Virginia

Jenkins's Brigade Col. Joseph Walker
*1st South Carolina • 2nd South Carolina Rifles • 5th South Carolina
6th South Carolina • 4th South Carolina Battalion • Palmetto South Carolina
Sharpshooters*

Kemper's Brigade Brig. Gen. J. L. Kemper
1st Virginia • 7th Virginia • 11th Virginia • 17th Virginia • 24th Virginia

Anderson's Brigade Col. George T. Anderson
1st Georgia Regulars • 7th Georgia • 8th Georgia • 9th Georgia • 11th Georgia

Artillery
Wise (VA) Artillery

WALKER'S DIVISION Brig. Gen. John Walker
Walker's Brigade Col. Van H. Manning; Col. E. D. Hall
*3rd Arkansas • 27th North Carolina • 46th North Carolina • 48th North Carolina
30th Virginia • French's (VA) Battery*

Ransom's Brigade Brig. Gen. Robert Ransom, Jr.
*24th North Carolina • 25th North Carolina • 35th North Carolina
49th North Carolina • Branch's (VA) Field Artillery*

HOOD'S DIVISION Brig. Gen. John Bell Hood
Hood's Brigade Col. William T. Wofford
18th Georgia • Hampton's Legion (SC) • 1st Texas • 4th Texas • 5th Texas

Law's Brigade Col. Evander M. Law
4th Alabama • 2nd Mississippi • 11th Mississippi • 6th North Carolina

Artillery Maj. B. W. Frobel
German Artillery (SC) • Palmetto Artillery (SC) • Rowan Artillery (NC)

Evans's Brigade Brig. Gen. Nathan G. Evans; Col. P. F. Stevens
*17th South Carolina • 18th South Carolina • 22nd South Carolina
23rd South Carolina • Holcombe (SC) Legion • Macbeth (SC) Artillery*

Artillery Col. J. B. Walton
Washington (LA) Artillery, 1st-4th Companies

Lee's Battalion Col. S. D. Lee
*Ashland (VA) Artillery • Bedford (VA) Artillery • Brooks (SC) Artillery
Eubank's (VA) Battery • Madison (LA) Light Artillery • Parker's (VA) Battery*

JACKSON'S COMMAND Maj. Gen. Thomas J. Jackson
EWELL'S DIVISION Brig. Gen. Alexander Lawton; Brig. Gen. Jubal Early
Lawton's Brigade Col. M. Douglass; Maj. J. H. Lowe; Col. John H. Lamar
*13th Georgia • 26th Georgia • 31st Georgia • 38th Georgia • 60th Georgia
61st Georgia*

Trimble's Brigade Col. James A. Walker
*15th Alabama • 12th Georgia • 21st Georgia • 21st North Carolina
1st North Carolina Battalion*

Early's Brigade Brig. Gen. Jubal Early; Col. William Smith
*13th Virginia • 25th Virginia • 31st Virginia • 44th Virginia
49th Virginia • 52nd Virginia • 58th Virginia*

Hays's Brigade Brig. Gen. Harry T. Hays
5th Louisiana • 6th Louisiana • 7th Louisiana • 8th Louisiana • 14th Louisiana

Artillery Maj. A. R. Courtney
Johnson's (VA) Battery • Louisiana Guard Artillery • First Maryland Battery
Staunton (VA) Artillery

JACKSON'S DIVISION Brig. Gen. John R. Jones; Brig. Gen. William Starke;
Col. Andrew Grigsby
Winder's Brigade Col. Andrew Grigsby; Lt. Col. R. D. Gardner;
Maj. H. J. Williams
4th Virginia • 5th Virginia • 27th Virginia • 33rd Virginia

Taliaferro's Brigade Col. James W. Jackson; Col. James L. Sheffield
47th Alabama • 48th Alabama • 23rd Virginia • 37th Virginia

Jones's Brigade Capt. John E. Penn; Capt. A. C. Page; Capt. R. W. Withers
21st Virginia • 42nd Virginia • 48th Virginia • 1st Virginia Battalion

Starke's Brigade Brig. Gen. William E. Starke; Col. Jesse M. Williams;
Col. Leroy A. Stafford; Col. Edmund Pendleton
1st Louisiana • 2nd Louisiana • 9th Louisiana • 10th Louisiana
15th Louisiana • 1st Louisiana Battalion

Artillery Maj. L. M. Shumaker
Alleghany (VA) Artillery • Danville (VA) Artillery • Lee (VA) Artillery
Rockbridge (VA) Artillery • Brockenbrough's (MD) Artillery

D. H. HILL'S DIVISION Maj. Gen. D. H. Hill
Ripley's Brigade Brig. Gen. Roswell S. Ripley; Col. George Doles
4th Georgia • 44th Georgia • 1st North Carolina • 3rd North Carolina

Rodes's Brigade Brig. Gen. Robert E. Rodes
3rd Alabama • 5th Alabama • 6th Alabama • 12th Alabama • 26th Alabama

Garland's Brigade Brig. Gen. Samuel Garland; Col. D. K. McRae
5th North Carolina • 12th North Carolina • 13th North Carolina
20th North Carolina • 23rd North Carolina

Anderson's Brigade Brig. Gen. George B. Anderson; Col. C. C. Tew;
Col. R. T. Bennett
2nd North Carolina • 4th North Carolina • 14th North Carolina • 30th North Carolina

Colquitt's Brigade Brig. Gen. Alfred Colquitt
13th Alabama • 6th Georgia • 23rd Georgia • 27th Georgia • 28th Georgia

Artillery Maj. C. F. Pierson
Jones's (VA) Battery • King William (VA) Artillery • Hardaway's (AL) Battery
Jeff Davis (AL) Artillery

HILL'S LIGHT DIVISION Maj. Gen. A. P. Hill
Branch's Brigade Brig. Gen. Lawrence O'Bryan Branch; Col. James H. Lane
7th North Carolina • 18th North Carolina • 28th North Carolina
33rd North Carolina • 37th North Carolina

Archer's Brigade Brig. Gen. James Archer; Col. Peter Turney
5th Alabama • 19th Georgia • 1st Tennessee (Provisional) • 7th Tennessee
14th Tennessee

Gregg's Brigade Brig. Gen. Maxcy Gregg
1st South Carolina (Provisional) • 1st South Carolina Rifles • 12th South Carolina
13th South Carolina • 14th South Carolina

Pender's Brigade Brig. Gen. William D. Pender; Col. R. H. Brewer
16th North Carolina • 22nd North Carolina • 34th North Carolina • 38th North Carolina

Fields's Brigade Col. John Brockenbrough
40th Virginia • 47th Virginia • 55th Virginia • 22nd Virginia

Thomas's Brigade Col. Edward L. Thomas
14th Georgia • 35th Georgia • 45th Georgia • 49th Georgia

Artillery
Fredericksburg (VA) Artillery • Pee Dee (SC) Artillery • Purcell (VA) Artillery
Crenshaw's (VA) Artillery • Letcher's (VA) Battery

CAVALRY Maj. Gen. James E. B. Stuart
Hampton's Brigade Brig. Gen. Wade Hampton
1st North Carolina • 2nd South Carolina • Cobb's (GA) Legion • Jeff Davis Legion

Lee's Brigade Brig. Gen. Fitzhugh Lee
1st Virginia • 3rd Virginia • 4th Virginia • 5th Virginia • 9th Virginia

Munford's Brigade Col. Thomas T. Munford
2nd Virginia • 6th Virginia • 7th Virginia • 12th Virginia • 17th Virginia Battalion

Horse Artillery Capt. John Pelham
Chew's (VA) Battery • Hart's (SC) Battery • Pelham's (VA) Battery

RESERVE ARTILLERY Brig. Gen. William Pendleton
Cutt's Battalion Lt. Col. A. S. Cutts
Blackshears's (GA) Battery • Patterson's (GA) Battery
Irwin (GA) Artillery • Ross's (GA) Battery • Lloyd's (NC) Battery

Jones's Battalion Maj. H. P. Jones
Turner's (VA) Battery • Orange (VA) Artillery • Morris (VA) Artillery
Wimbish's (VA) Battery

Unattached
Magruder Artillery • Cutshaw's (VA) Battery

Suggested Reading

**The Maryland Campaign of September 1862
(South Mountain, Antietam, Shepherdstown
Ford and the End of the Campaign)
Ezra Carman, edited by Tom Clemens**
Savas Beatie (2010, 2012, 2016)
ISBN: 978-1-61121-114-6
Ezra Carman was a veteran of Antietam, and the first
official historian of the Antietam Battlefield Board. He
compiled the first official history of the battle, based off
of years of research and correspondence with veterans.
Antietam historian Tom Clemens has recently edited
Carman's work, providing key footnotes and context
for the narrative of the campaign and battle. The
three volumes stands as the definitive works on the
battle and campaign today.

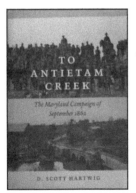

**To Antietam Creek
D. Scott Hartwig**
Johns Hopkins University Press (2012)
ISBN: 978-1-4214-0631-2
An intensive yet highly readable work, Hartwig's
weighty volume provides an extremely in-depth
account of the Maryland campaign in the lead-
up to Antietam, taking the reader all the way up
through the night of September 16. His analysis of
the commanding generals, the armies themselves,
and the events of the campaign is recommended for
anyone seeking a deeper understanding of how these
two armies arrived at Antietam. It is essential reading
for understanding the Maryland campaign.